ABORIGINAL ADOLESCENCE

■ A volume in the series
Adolescents in a Changing World
EDITED BY BEATRICE B. WHITING AND
JOHN W. M. WHITING

Project advisors:

Irven DeVore
Carol Gilligan
George W. Goethals
Jerome Kagan
Robert A. LeVine

Aboriginal Adolescence

Maidenhood in an Australian Community

Victoria Katherine Burbank

RUTGERS UNIVERSITY PRESS

New Brunswick and London

Library of Congress Cataloging-in-Publication Data

Burbank, Victoria Katherine.
   Aboriginal adolescence.

   (Adolescents in a changing world ; v. 2)
   Bibliography: p.
   Includes index.
   1. Australian aborigines—Social life and customs.
2. Adolescent girls—Australia—Sexual behavior.
3. Marriage—Australia. I. Title. II. Series.
GN663.B88   1988   305.2'35'0899915094   87-20505
ISBN 0-8135-1286-7

British Cataloging-in-Publication
information available

Material from this book has been previously published as "Premarital Sex Norms: Cultural
Interpretations in an Australian Aboriginal Community" in *Ethnos* 15, no. 2 (1987), and is
reproduced by permission of the American Anthropological Association.

■ Contents

■ Foreword

to Adolescents in a Changing World series
BEATRICE B. WHITING
JOHN W. M. WHITING

Few periods of the human life cycle have generated as much interest, or as much concern, as adolescence. The psychological, behavioral, and physical changes that occur at puberty are dramatic and have been the focus of much research by psychologists, educators, and sociologists. The study of adolescence has recently become a priority research topic among many private and government granting agencies, largely as a response to the increase in adjustment problems among American adolescents: alcohol and drug abuse, teenage suicide, juvenile delinquency, and teenage pregnancy. The study of adolescence is important not only because there is an urgent need to understand the socially destructive aspects of this life stage, but also because knowledge of this life stage can contribute greatly to a general understanding of the social, psychological, and physical aspects of human development in our own and other cultures.

Only recently have anthropologists turned their attention to the study of adolescence. Other than Margaret Mead's classic work *Coming of Age in Samoa,* few anthropologists have entered the field with the primary intention of conducting research on the adolescent experience in another society. While many ethnographies contain data on initiation rites, age grades, marriage practices, and premarital sexual behavior, all of which are important to the study of adolescence, the reporting of these topics has often been anecdotal in nature. For this reason we have organized and edited this series of volumes describing adolescence in seven different societies. These works are the product of years of fieldwork, data analysis, and writing by the staff and fellows of the Harvard Adolescence Project. These ethnographies will contribute to our knowledge of human development in other societies and perhaps stimulate similar research in other cultures in this fascinating stage of life.

Our interest in the cross-cultural study of adolescence is a natural outgrowth of our work on child development. Over the years we have had the opportunity to study the social behavior of children in a variety of cultures. Either individually or together, we have made field observations on American Indian children, the Kwoma of New Guinea, the Yoruba of Nigeria, the Kikuyu of Kenya, and preschool children in the United States. We have also directed several cross-cultural projects on child socialization, including the Six Cultures study and the socialization part of Florence and Clyde Kluckhohn's study of values in the American Southwest. Most recently, as directors of the Child Development Research Unit of the University of Nairobi, we have had the opportunity to explore the patterns of family life among nine different cultural groups in Kenya.

Our involvement in these studies has provided us with a rich, cross-cultural data base on child development. We have learned that although there are many dramatic differences in the behavior of children across cultures, the common features are also striking. Some of these commonalities are particularly relevant to the study of adolescence. For example, in none of the cultures we have studied were boys and girls adequately prepared for the sudden surge of sex hormones that announce the onset of puberty. We have discovered that, in many respects, the socialization of children is counterproductive preparation for this event. Presumably as a consequence of the incest taboo, free and frank talk about sex is inhibited between parents and children. In none of the societies we have studied, nor in any other that we know of, do adults copulate in public. As a result, the sex act, from the child's perspective, is shrouded in secrecy and mystery.

Although adolescence requires many changes in the lifestyles of girls and boys, the cultural scripts for social and economic behavior are more clearly formulated and more easily transmitted than those for sexual behavior. Since in late childhood same-sex companions predominate, learning appropriate heterosexual behavior and finding an appropriate mate are important tasks for adolescents. The hormonal changes that take place also require significant adjustments in self-image and emotions. Our studies focus on the changes in friendship formation, peer group relations, parent-child interactions, school achievement, self-image, and cognitive development.

In 1978, working with Robert Levine at the Laboratory of Human Development at the Harvard Graduate School of Education, we sponsored a postdoctoral fellow, Carol Worthman, to initiate a study of Kikuyu adolescence. A biological anthropologist interested in human growth, Carol Worthman conducted her research in the community of Ngeca, Kenya, a site where we had previously done fieldwork on Kikuyu children. While Worthman's study concentrated primarily upon the biological parameters of adolescent growth, it also focused upon the relationship between physical development and cognitive/behavioral changes. The success of this research proved to us the feasibility of conducting a multifactorial study of adolescence, thus laying the foundation for a larger cross-cultural investigation. In addition, our previous successes with the cross-cultural study of children convinced us that a similar design could be utilized for the study of adolescence.

In order to ensure the multidisciplinary nature of the project, we persuaded a group of our colleagues at Harvard to join us in planning the project. Clinical and personality psychology were represented by Carol Gilligan and George Goethals, child development by Jerome Kagan, biological anthropology by Peter Ellison and Irven DeVore, and psychological anthropology by Robert LeVine and the two of us. Irven DeVore agreed to accept the role of senior investigator.

We all agreed that the Harvard Adolescence Project should consist of field studies carried out in different regions of the world in cultures representing varying degrees of complexity. We also agreed that our sampling universe in each field site should consist of some bounded microcommunity, such as a band, a hamlet, or a neighborhood. We had used such a unit in our cross-cultural studies of child rearing, calling it a PSU (primary sampling unit). Briefly defined, a PSU is a small group of households (thirty to forty) which sets itself off from the larger

society in such a way that it has some sort of group identifica-
tion, shares frequent face-to-face interaction among its members, and possesses temporal and/or spatial stability. The PSU
has the advantage of being the most appropriate social unit for
using standard ethnographic research techniques, such as par-
ticipant observation and informant interviewing.

Knowing that most ethnographic studies require a prolonged "settling-in" period during which the researcher learns
the native language and becomes acquainted with the members
of the community, we decided to select experienced field-
workers who had already done extensive research in some other
culture and who would be willing to return to that society to
carry out a study of adolescence.

To implement the above plans, we applied for and received
a post-doctoral training grant from the National Institute of
Mental Health (grant number MH14066-06,07,08) that would
support ten fellows for two years each. Additional support for
data analysis was provided by the William T. Grant Foundation.
The fellows chosen were Douglas D. and Wannie Wibulswasdi
Anderson, Victoria K. Burbank, Richard G. Condon, Douglas A.
and Susan Schaefer Davis, Marida C. Hollos, Phillip F. Leis,
Mitchell S. Ratner, and Carol Worthman. The field sites listed
from east to west included the Inuit (Copper Eskimo) of Holman located on Victoria Island in the Central Canadian Arctic;
the Australian Aborigines of Mangrove located in Arnhem Land,
Northern Australia; the Thai Muslim of Nipa Island located on
the southwestern coast of Thailand; the Kikuyu of Ngeca located in the Central Province of Kenya, twenty miles north of
Nairobi; the Ijo of Ebiama and Opuware located in the central
part of the Niger Delta in southern Nigeria; the Romanians of
Baisoara located in the foothills of the inner Carpathian moun-
tains; and the Moroccan Muslim of Zawiya located in North
Central Morocco.

During the initial training period, a series of seminars were
held in which the project's staff members and postdoctoral fellows gave presentations on topics relating to adolescent development. These seminar presentations proved helpful not only in
identifying important issues in the field of adolescent development, but in assisting the project directors and fellows in developing research methods with cross-cultural applications. In

addition, the information and insights provided by the research fellows on their particular field sites helped immensely in developing a research strategy that could be applied reasonably in all the research settings.

It was clear from the beginning of our discussions that no single definition of adolescence would serve all purposes. Since we were approaching adolescence from a multidisciplinary perspective, both the physiological and sociocultural definitions of adolescence were necessary to incorporate into the research methodology. Our basic assumption was that while the physiological changes that occur at adolescence are universal to all human populations, the social and cultural reactions to these physical maturational changes are not. Thus, while one culture may celebrate puberty publicly, subjecting individuals to a series of initiation rites and expecting a consequent change in the behavior of initiates, in other societies the physiological markers are a private matter.

Physiological definitions of adolescence, such as the interval between the beginning of the growth spurt and the attainment of full skeletal maturity or the interval between adrenarche and the attainment of full fecundity, could ideally be objectively measured through hormone assays in all the field sites. Theoretically, such physiological measures would provide the most valid comparison of adolescent maturation across cultures. Unfortunately, the logistical problems associated with such data collection as well as the social constraints encountered in most of the field sites prevented this type of data from being collected. (Only in Ngeca was the field-worker able to make such hormone assays.) As a result, we decided to concentrate upon the growth spurt for our physiological measure. Thus, the children at each field site were measured twice during the fieldwork period—once near the beginning and a second time near the end of the study period. From these measurements of height and weight the field-workers were able to calculate a growth rate for each child and from this determine his or her status with respect to physical maturation.

These measures of physical maturation were essential to obtain since we hoped to examine the effect the maturation process had upon such things as friendship formation, cognitive development, peer group relations, self-image, gender identity, and so forth. For example, does the young girl who has menstruated for the first time have a different self-image than the girl who is two to three years past menarche? Does the young boy who has just entered the growth spurt have a different gender identity than a boy who has attained full skeletal maturity? By combining our measures of physical maturation (as an independent variable) with other types of social and psychological data (as dependent variables) we hoped to address these questions for all the societies under investigation.

It was much more difficult, however, to operationalize a sociocultural definition of adolescence. Since we assumed that societies utilized different strategies for identifying and managing adolescence, it was not feasible to develop precise definitions that had any degree of cross-cultural comparability. In the end, we decided upon a broad definition: the transitional period between the end of childhood and the attainment of adult social status. This broad definition made it essential for our field-workers to examine local definitions of adolescence, which we assumed would vary among the seven cultures in our study. Thus, where one culture might rely upon physical maturation to mark the individual's transition into adolescence, another culture might rely solely upon chronological age as the criterion for entry into this stage. It was also theoretically possible that a society might not even reocgnize or name a transitional period between childhood and adulthood. As a result, the challenge to our field-workers was to remain as sensitive as possible to indigenous "folk theories" of human maturation.

To solve the practical problem of choosing a sample of subjects to be studied at each field site, we decided to select a single physiological marker that was transculturally recognized. The mean age of menarche was chosen for this purpose. For many of our field sites, an estimate of the mean age of menarche was available from previously published demographic and/or growth studies. For those field sites lacking such published estimates, the field-workers would have to collect data from postmenarcheal girls and women, which could then be averaged to produce an estimate of the mean age of menarche. This estimate could then be used as the anchor point for the selection of a study population that would include a group of preadoleàscents as well as a group of adolescents. Previous research on adolescent growth indicates that a ten-year interval centered on the mean age of menarche will include both the beginning of physiological adolescence for most of the early-maturing females and the end of physiological adolescence for the most late-maturing females. Thus, for middle-class American girls for whom the mean age of menarche is thirteen, the catchment period would run from eight to eighteen years of age. Although there is no equivalent marker of physical maturation for males, we took advantage of the fact that males mature about a year later than females, and added a year to the interval used for females.

Ideally, we believed the sample size should range from eighty to ninety individuals. All of these individuals would be subjected to our physical measures of height and weight, while smaller subsamples would be subjected to clinical interviews, cognitive testing, behavioral observations, and a number of other structured and unstructured interviews designed to examine the social and psychological aspects of adolescence. Sample and subsample sizes would, of course, vary from one field site to the next, depending upon such things as community size and accessibility of informants. (The actual problems encountered in sample selection and informant interviewing were unique to each setting and are discussed in each of the volumes in this series.)

At the end of the training period, the staff and fellows produced a detailed field guide for the cross-cultural study of adolescence. This field guide represented the consensus of the research group concerning types of data to be collected and the manner of their collection. The document was developed in order to ensure a maximum degree of comparability among the field sites included in the study. The manual also suggested specific hypotheses to be tested and the methods for doing so. In line with the multidisciplinary focus of the project, we decided to draw upon the theories and hypotheses of a number of disciplines. The field manual included detailed discussions of research methodology (site selection, sampling procedures, geneaological and demographic data collection, psychological testing procedures, and methods for making physical measurements) as well as discussions on the substantive topics to be covered (parent-child relations, peer group formation, friendship, games and play activities, sexual activity, cognitive development, schooling, religious activities, pair-bonding, rites of passage, work, daily activities, and deviance).

With the training sessions over and the field guide complete, the researchers departed for their respective field sites, where the average stay was from nine to twelve months. The project directors and researchers maintained as much contact with one another as was possible, given the isolation of some of the field sites. In some cases, letters took several months to go halfway around the world. Nevertheless, all of us felt it important for the researchers to stay in contact with one another in order to share problems encountered and modifications made in the research design.

By February of 1983, all of the researchers reconvened at Harvard to begin the task of comparing and analyzing the extensive data that had been collected. Again, a series of seminars were held in which information was exchanged among all the project's participants. This phase of the research proved to be most exciting and stimulating as we saw the ultimate goals of the research begin to fall in place. Our research fellows returned with interesting observations and innovative ideas which were freely shared.

In the process of analyzing this extensive cross-cultural data base, all of us agreed that the first order of business should be the writing of a series of ethnographies providing detailed descriptions of the adolescent experience in each of the cultures. These would provide the necessary framework upon which later theoretical and comparative papers could be built.

Given the rapid rate of social change occurring throughout the world in general and in the field sites of the Harvard Adolescence Project in particular, we have decided to call this series Adolescents in a Changing World. With the publication of these ethnographically rich volumes by the fellows of the Harvard Adolescence Project, we hope that our cross-cultural and multidisciplinary examination of adolescence will contribute a much needed perspective to this fascinating stage of human development.

■ Acknowledgments

This monograph is based on data derived from two periods of research in Australia and is the result of several years of effort. During these years I have been helped and encouraged by many people whom I would like to acknowledge here.

First, I would like to thank the people of Mangrove, young and old, Aboriginal and white, who saw to my comfort and education during my two stays in their community. I am especially grateful to the adolescents and adults who acted as informants. What interest this book may have is due in large part to their willingness to share their thoughts and feelings with me.

Acknowledgment is due to the many staff members of the Australian Institue of Aboriginal Studies for their instruction and friendly assistance. I would particularly like to thank Peter Ucko for his assistance and encouragement beyond the call of duty during my first trip into the field. I would also like to thank Jeffrey Heath for outlining for me the grammar of the Aboriginal language used at Mangrove. Thanks are also due to the staff of the Darwin Public Library for their helpful responses to my many inquiries.

In Sydney, Canberra, Katherine, and Darwin, I was helped, housed, advised, and cheered by Janice Reid, Francesca Merlan, Gillian Cowlishaw, Les Hiatt, Margaret Clunies-Ross, Jeremy Beckett, Basil Sansom, Nancy Williams, Leslie Brown, the Henry and Riche families, Dick and Diane Barwick, Myrna and Bob Tonkinson, Anne and Allan Walker, Chris Devonport,

Shirley Hendy, Annie Thompson, Vivienne Sobek, Annette Hamilton, Nicky Modjeska, Betty Meehan, Warwick and Glenneth Dix, Harold Scheffler, Peter Willis, and Joan Smedley.

In the midst of my second stay at Mangrove I very much appreciated a visit from Irven and Nancy DeVore and the gifts and news that they brought from the outside world. I would also like to thank my parents, Monroe and Katherine Burbank, for making sure that my mailbox was never empty on mail days.

Back in the United States my efforts at data analysis and writing were supported by the help, encouragement, and friendship of Sara Harkness, Charlie Super, Mitzi Goheen, Nadine Peacock, Barb Smuts, Lila Abu-Lughod, Lucy and Jeremy Murray-Brown, Cathy Lutz, Judy Strauch, Fran Aaron, Nancy Harvey, Scott Rushforth, Pat Draper, Henry Harpending, Carol Worthman, Max Katz, Dan Rosenberg, Theodore Nadelson, and James Chisholm.

For their careful reading and thoughtful comments on the various drafts of this manuscript I want to acknowledge and thank Warren Shapiro, Carol Worthman, Pat Draper, Martin Etter, Francesca Merlan, Janice Reid, Phil Leis, John and Beatrice Whiting, Susan Davis, Nancy DeVore, James Chisholm, Pam Stern, and Wanni Anderson. This volume is better than it might have been thanks to conversations with Annette Hamilton and Fred Myers and the comments of an anonymous reviewer for Rutgers University Press.

The help and teaching of the many people who worked on the Harvard Adolescence Project must be acknowledged here. In particular I would like to thank Doug Davis and Rick Condon for their help on the computer, Nancy Hendricks for teaching me how to word process, and Masako Iguchi and Nancy Black for countless acts of assistance.

I would like to thank the principals of the Adolescence Project, Irven DeVore and John and Beatrice Whiting, for allowing me to benefit from the experience of their many years of anthropological research. I would also like to acknowledge my debt, and the debt of this volume, to the teaching of Barbara C. Ayres, Margaret K. Bacon, Warren Shapiro, and Janet Siskind.

Access to the records of the missionary society of Mangrove and permission to quote them in these pages are very much appreciated.

This research was supported by the National Institute of Mental Health, the William T. Grant Foundation, the Australian Institute of Aboriginal Studies, the Northern Territory Department of Health, and the Harry Frank Guggenheim Foundation.

ABORIGINAL
ADOLESCENCE

1
Introduction

This analysis of female adolescence in an Australian Aboriginal community focuses on adolescent sexual behavior, marriage, and the conflict between adult expectations and adolescent behavior in these domains. It continues a trend begun many years ago in anthropology: the cross-cultural comparison of human development. Few comparative studies, however, have focused on the stage of adolescence. Indeed, it is hard to find such a study since Margaret Mead's *Coming of Age in Samoa* (1928), a work pursued in the late 1920s. Due to the dearth of comparative material on adolescence even in the anthropological literature, my research in the settlement of Mangrove was initially guided by the question, What is the adolescent experience in this community?[1]

All humans develop from immature members of the species into adults, and all human communities must take into account a relatively prolonged period of development that includes the appearance of secondary sex characteristics and the beginnings of reproductive capacities. Thanks to the cross-cultural work of Alice Schlegel, we know that cultural recognition of adolescence is widespread (1983). But, as stated in the foreword to this book, the particular manner in which this stage of human development is conceptualized in a given society is important data for understanding adolescence in that society.

Undoubtedly, the conceptualizations of a group affect the expectations and behavior of the adolescents in that group. Thus, I, like my fellow project field-workers, went into the field with only an orienting definition of adolescence as a transitional period between childhood and adulthood. Similarly, I began field research with the charter to operate largely in terms of the culturally defined concept of adolescence.

ADOLESCENCE AT MANGROVE

Adolescence is a life stage that is recognized in the language and the behavior of the people of Mangrove. Mangrove is a multilingual community. Its members speak an Australian language, Kriol—an English-based Creole—and an Aboriginal version of English. What Westerners might regard as adolescent girls are referred to as *ngalanyjinyung* in the indigenous language. In Kriol adolescent females are called "young girls" or "single girls." They retain these labels when the Aboriginal speaker uses English. Adolescent boys are *wulmurinyung* and "young boys" or "single boys."

A young girl begins to be such when her budding breasts are first noticed.[2] A boy becomes a young boy as his body approaches adult size, his facial hair becomes visible, and his voice begins to deepen. Marriage and the birth of children bring this stage to an end for both males and females.

The congruence of these Aboriginal, Kriol, and English labels for adolescent boys and girls belies, however, the radical changes that appear to have taken place in the duration and content of this life stage since the Aborigines of Mangrove abandoned their nomadic past for life on a settlement. It is one of these changes and its significance for an understanding of adolescence as a human phenomenon that is the central theme of this description of female adolescence: the introduction of a period of "maidenhood."

MAIDENHOOD AT MANGROVE

Maidenhood, as recently redefined by John Whiting (Whiting, Burbank, and Ratner 1986), is the period between the beginning of fertility and motherhood, two events that are normally, from a cross-cultural perspective, marked by menarche and marriage.[3] The period of maidenhood varies across societies. In some, for example, there is no period of maidenhood because girls are married before menarche and the onset of fertility. This was the case in many parts of Aboriginal Australia, including the area around Mangrove. In other societies, particularly complex Western ones, the period of maidenhood extends for a number of years. For example, the average duration of the period between menarche and marriage in the United States is nearly eight years (Whiting, Burbank, and Ratner 1982). Today Aboriginal girls at Mangrove pass through a period of maidenhood between three and four years in duration, for they begin menstruating between the ages of thirteen and fourteen but do not, on the average, marry until the age of about seventeen.[4]

In but a generation or two, the people of Mangrove have witnessed the introduction of a period of maidenhood into their society which lasts for three or four years. At least in theory, the premenarcheal marriage age of previous times fit well with the marriage system characterized as it was by arranged unions of partners structurally defined as correct. The marriage system, in turn, was consonant with a social structure based on statuses acquired from the individual's mother and father. Aboriginal models of social organization still guide the perceptions of the people of Mangrove. However, much of the courtship and sexual behavior that takes place during the newly created period of maidenhood subverts institutions formed by the indigenous rules. Indeed, the institutional aspect of the past marriage system is now largely defunct. The accompanying values, however, are clearly still alive, at least in the adult segment of the population. The conflict between adult expectations and adolescent behavior, arising in large part from the recent introduction of maidenhood, is perhaps one of the most critical issues at Mangrove today and thus an apt focus for this exploration of Aboriginal female adolescence.[5]

A girl who is married before menarche should experience the period of transition from childhood to adulthood very differently from a girl who spends these years as an unmarried female. Similarly, adult members of societies characterized by different lengths of maidenhood can be expected to have very

different concerns about their adolescents. Premarital pregnancy, for example, can hardly be a problem in a community
where most girls are married before menarche. This monograph focuses on the concerns and experiences of Aboriginal
adults and adolescents that accompany the relatively prolonged
period of maidenhood at Mangrove.

THE REGULATION OF FEMALE SEXUALITY

Many cultural anthropologists today believe that the social
arrangements and behavior of any group of people can be understood largely in terms of their self-perceptions and theories
about themselves (see, for example, Agar 1973; D'Andrade
1984; Goodenough 1970; Keesing 1974; Lutz and White 1986).
This volume exemplifies the validity of this orientation. But the
Aboriginal women and adolescents who speak throughout this
work are, perhaps, exceptionally insightful observers of human
behavior. Their conceptualizations not only provide a guide for
understanding adolescent behavior at Mangrove, but may also
provide a broader understanding of female adolescence as a
general human phenomenon.

These observers and theoreticians of human behavior at
Mangrove have not addressed themselves to many of the questions and problems of adolescence that concern some of us in
the Western world. They are not concerned with drug addic-
tion, nor with teenage drivers, nor with the cognitive development and academic strivings that preoccupy so many. Their
concerns, at least as this volume presents them, are focused on
but one aspect of adolescence; they are concerned about the
consequences of unregulated female sexuality.[6] This issue of
adolescence is not only one of our concerns, but a concern of
universal proportions (Murdock 1949, 260).

Unlike the human male, the human female "develops
nearly all her secondary sex characteristics to their fullest extent before acquiring her fertility" (Richardson and Short 1978,
21 in Lancaster 1986, 21). Lancaster suggests that this characteristic of the adolescent female allows her to gain experiences
that may be critical to her success as a mother; she may participate in the adult female's social and sexual role before she is

burdened with the responsibilities of motherhood (Lancaster 1986, 21; see also Short 1976). Yet human sexuality has an "enormous potential" to disrupt society, and societies must, consequently, act to minimize this possibility (Broude 1981, 633). The human female's early ability to practice her adult sexual role is a potential problem for any human group.

At one time it appears that the Aborigines of Mangrove attempted to regulate female sexuality, at least as far as adolescent females were concerned, by marrying them off before they were sexually mature. Thus ideally, by the time a female was likely to be interested in sexual activity and could reproduce, she had been placed with a male that her community deemed an appropriate sexual partner and father of her children. Today, however, premenarcheal marriage as one means of controlling female sexuality is no longer available to the people of Mangrove.[7]

Today, like most adolescents in Western society, the adolescent girls of Mangrove experience a period of maidenhood. Unlike Western society, however, this is a new and disjunctive social arrangement. The newly prolonged maidenhood of Mangrove's adolescent girls clearly contributes to behavior that is not in accord with the system of adult, if not adolescent, values. These sources of disarray in the social arrangements of a people who are experiencing afresh what we have long been accustomed to provide us with a relatively unimpeded view of potential consequences of prolonged maidenhood. It is likely, for example, that this disarray makes the women and young girls of Mangrove such acute observers, for they are faced with a troubling and unprecedented phenomenon for which there are few if any well- established cultural formulas.

INFORMANTS

This monograph is based primarily on nine months of fieldwork in the Aboriginal community of Mangrove, undertaken between March and December of 1981. It is also based on material collected during a previous eighteen-month field trip to this community in 1977 and 1978.

Between March and December 1981, there were approximately sixty young girls residing at Mangrove. I say approximately because people come and go in this Aboriginal community; at times there may have been several more than this number, at times less. For fifty-five of these girls, it was possible to obtain data such as birth dates, marital status, and reproductive history. This group is, consequently, regarded as the basic sample in the pages that follow. However, while this sample provides a baseline of information, caselike studies of three young girls are the primary vehicle of this presentation.

The adolescent girls of Mangrove are usually "shy" of Western strangers, and I found them to be shy with me. As the quotations around the word above indicate, "shy" is an Aboriginal concept. Its behavioral connotations include silence and gaze aversion. Shyness is frequently associated with female adolescents. For example, it was said that adolescent girls did not take part in funeral dancing because they were "shy." The word also encapsulates behavior that is expected in the presence of strangers. In spite of my previous stay in the community, I was a stranger to the majority of adolescent girls. Exacerbating this problem is the Aboriginal response to the question—a basic tool of anthropological research. From the Aboriginal perspective, the question, especially from a relative stranger, often appears to be an unacceptable form of behavior. Small children, who are not expected to know how to behave properly, ask questions. Adults who do so generally do it with some apology, especially if the question is at all personal in nature (see also von Sturmer 1981; Reid 1983, 53, 112). Adolescent girls were quite happy to spend time with me, often for hours on end, as long as I did not ask them questions and as long as they did not have to talk to me. "Establishing rapport" in such circumstances consisted largely of placing myself in a position where I could become less of a stranger, of allowing time to pass, and of waiting for informants to select themselves. Eventually, three did, the three young girls on whose stories this description is based: Marguerite, Kay, and Nora.

Marguerite and I spent hours together during the time that I was at Mangrove. On my previous field trip, her mother, Lily, had been a major informant. When I returned, I worked briefly with Lily again, and then passed on, seemingly quite naturally, to work with Marguerite. At first, when Lily and I worked together sitting under a cashew tree next to their house, Lily would call upon Marguerite to fill in gaps in her memory. We moved from that to working as a group of three as Marguerite moved over to join us on our blanket under the tree. One day Lily left such a session after the first few questions. After that, the expectations of all seemed to be that when I appeared at the little house it was to work with Marguerite. In addition to our work sessions, Marguerite would visit me, usually several times a week, bringing news of her own and other's current affairs. She was my major source of information on adolescence at Mangrove.

I spent less time with Kay, an adolescent girl who worked as a teaching assistant. Our acquaintance, which began early in the study, was interrupted by the death of Kay's father. Aside from one interview, we conversed very little in these early months. In the latter third of the field stay, however, she agreed to a series of interviews for the study. It was during this period that she became a regular informant.

Nora's mother, Rosalind, had also been an important informant on my first visit to Mangrove and became the major adult informant for this study. When we worked together, and on Rosalind's frequent visits to my house, Nora was present more often than not. In the latter third of the study, Nora also agreed to participate and completed a series of nine interview schedules and tasks.

In addition to these three girls, I was occasionally able to hold conversations with a few other adolescent girls. Thanks to the postprimary schoolteachers, I was able to interview groups of two to four adolescent schoolgirls on four occasions. Adolescent visitors also occasionally volunteered information about themselves or fellow adolescents. By and large, however, my understanding of female adolescence at Mangrove, and this volume, is based on interviews and conversations with Marguerite, Kay, and Nora.

These three, largely self-selected, young girls are a fortuitous sample insofar as their lives appear to exemplify those of many others. They are very much like their peers in terms of the issues confronting the young girls of Mangrove today and in their responses to them. This is certainly the case with those issues associated with the current prolonged period of maidenhood that they all experience. In later chapters, this representativeness may be judged by the reader since the case material of the three is presented in the context of material gathered on other adolescents.

One way in which these girls might have been more representative is in their ages. Both Marguerite and Kay were eighteen during most of 1981; Nora was fifteen. The fifty-five sample adolescents ranged in age, however, from eleven to twenty. Eleven- and twelve-year-old girls were pointed to as "young girls" on the grounds that their breasts were "shooting out." But it was not until the age of thirteen and fourteen that young girls were known to begin dating, an activity that precipitates much of the intergenerational conflict at Mangrove. Thus, while the three girls do not represent the younger segment of the adolescent sample, that segment is not directly involved in the issues with which this description is concerned.

Insofar as Kay had a job she is unrepresentative of the majority of adolescent girls. During the field period only six of the fifty-five worked, and only three of these for most of the nine months. However, Kay's occupation did not prevent her from experiencing her period of maidenhood in much the same manner as her unemployed peers.

Informants generally agreed that the end of female adolescence was signaled by marriage and the birth of children. Yet these same informants often referred to young females who were married and had one child as "young girls." I asked about this use of the term. The answers I received indicate that people consider longevity when they think about a person's age stage. Informants did not, for example, say that these females would cease to be young girls when they had more children, but rather indicated that although they were married and had a child they were still young. The Aborigines of Mangrove have not, until recently, calculated age in terms of years, and contemporary usage of chronology is often idiosyncratic. For example, a woman told me that she thought she was thirty-two years old until the European secretary, with access to the birth records, told her she was twenty-nine. An adolescent who was to turn nineteen on her next birthday told me she would be turning twenty-one. Aborigines do, however, appear to take into account how long someone has lived, and this calculation appears to affect their determination of whether or not a female is a "woman" or a "young girl." For this reason, the sample of fifty-five includes females who are married and who, like Nora, have a child.

This volume focuses on female adolescence. That I was all but unable to work with the adolescent boys at Mangrove reflects a major theme of Aboriginal life and of Aboriginal adolescence: the segregation of the sexes. Although the separation of the sexes is not always rigid or complete, adolescent males and adolescent females usually formed distinct groups. As a woman alone, working without benefit of research assistants, it was usually inappropriate for me to be with adolescent males. Male adolescents, however, were often the topic of female adolescents' conversation. I was also able to observe some of their behavior, but not in a systematic manner. However, most critically for the kind of analysis I present here, my opportunities to hold conversations with adolescent males were rare, and these were even more rarely substantive. Consequently, this description of adolescent life in the community of Mangrove must be confined almost entirely to female adolescence, and thus to only a part of the story.

Adults also provided data for this work. Ten Aboriginal women and two Aboriginal men were interviewed about adolescent behavior. Six of these were mothers or guardians of adolescent girls, including Kay's mother's sister and the mothers of Marguerite and Nora. A number of whites were also interviewed. These include the five postprimary schoolteachers, the town clerk, minister, nursing sister, an area police officer, the settlement's welfare officer, and a former mission superintendent. This work also relies on material I gathered in 1977 and 1978 (see Burbank 1980). Informants for these years include fourteen Aboriginal women, three Aboriginal men, and several missionaries.

Although I spent the first eight months of my first year at Mangrove studying the Aboriginal language, I was never able to work in it and instead relied primarily on the English-based Creole that I learned with relative ease. In 1981, finding that my Kriol was very rusty and that adolescents addressed me in English (suggesting, perhaps, an initial equation between me and the white schoolteachers), I conversed and worked with them in that language.

THE BOOK

Underlying the recent Western accretions of the settlement is a culture whose history diverged from ours at least forty thousand years ago. But Mangrove cannot be identified as an example of a non-Western community without some discussion of how Westernized it has become and yet how Aboriginal it remains. Chapter 2 includes such a discussion. It also introduces the reader to Marguerite, Nora, and Kay and to various aspects of their lives on the settlement. Chapter 3 presents the historical and cultural factors that form a major basis of adult expectations about marriage. It describes the ideal model of marriage and the apparent changes occurring since Mangrove was established. A discussion of the marriages of the three girls' mothers and mothers' mothers demonstrates the rules and conditions of marriage in the recent past. In chapter 4, adolescent expectations about men and marriage are presented. The conflict between generations that arises from adolescent behavior is also detailed, as are the strategies employed by each generation in their battle over marriage. The implications of adolescent behavior with respect to sex and marriage are discussed in the concluding chapter.

■ 2
The Research Setting

A visitor's first glimpse of Mangrove usually comes as the twin engine Fokker circles the settlement prior to landing. There, suddenly, in the midst of a sparse eucalypt forest, scrub-covered sand dunes, mangrove swamp, and ocean are the roofs of houses, school buildings, the general store, clinic, and church. With a large river on its right, the plane, one of the biweekly flights from Darwin, some three hundred miles away, is ready to land on the packed dirt strip about a mile from the village. As it does, several vehicles, a red pickup and a yellow Land Rover among them, arrive in a swirl of orange dust from the gravel road laid down on top of the sandy terrain.

The passengers disembark from the plane, are ushered into the vehicles by their black and white drivers, and take their seats amid the sacks of mail, school supplies, and crates of lettuce that have also been brought on the flight. Once loaded, a couple of the vehicles immediately head for the settlement, but others remain, waiting, as law requires, until the plane is once again airborne on the last leg of its journey to a neighboring settlement just fifty miles away. Then they, too, turn and head down the road.

Within moments they are entering the Aboriginal village, driving down the main road. Here are the houses that go with the roofs the visitors first saw from the air. Some are not unlike houses from the manicured suburbs of Darwin, though this impression is somewhat belied by the stained exteriors, broken windows, and torn screens that are seen on some. Painted a variety of pastel shades, they range from new to dilapidated. Here and there is a brush shelter, a simple frame of tree limbs with a leafy roof, or a canvas tent that is, to judge by the tables, chairs, pots and pans, clothing, and flour barrels that surround it, somebody's home. Small fires smolder in many of the yards, some of clean raked sand, others littered with soft drink cans, empty sugar bags, and children's toys. The smell of smoke mingles with the smell of the sea, which can be seen just yards from the houses beyond the road. Men and women are gathered around the fires or in groups sitting under the coconut or cashew trees that shade some of the houses from the glare of the noonday sun. A woman stands and calls to a group of children playing by the house next door, just twenty or thirty feet away.

The vehicle drives slowly now, at twenty kilometers an hour, giving the groups of children playing in the road plenty of time to get out of the way. A small girl wobbles past on a bicycle and a dog moves out of the vehicle's path. The shouts of children playing with a soccer ball are echoed by the raucous crows fighting over the garbage in an overflowing barrel by the side of the road.

After proceeding along the road for just under a quarter of a mile, the vehicles turn away from the ocean and follow the road a few hundred feet up the incline of a sandhill. They stop at the top and the visitors get out in front of a complex of three buildings: the "office," which contains the bank, the settlement's one radio telephone, and the town clerk's office; the general store known as the "shop"; and the council hall, whose graffiti-scarred walls and broken louvered windows give it a deserted aspect. To their backs is a large white wooden billboard that is, in fact, the outdoor movie screen. The visitors are facing a tall tower of metal struts that houses the settlement's siren, lifting it well above the roof of the office so that its call to work can be heard throughout the settlement. It is here, at the base of the siren, that they are met by the school personnel, independent council workers, or missionaries whom they have come to visit.

With their hosts or hostesses by their sides, the visitors now walk along a road that runs from the office along the crest of the sandhill, away from the village they have just been driven through, in the direction of the "missionarea." They walk past the large complex of nine school buildings, past the clinic with a long veranda across its front and a red cross painted on its rooftop, past the rectory of the minister and his wife that backs on the barnlike church, and past a sixty-foot water tower upon whose platform several adolescent boys sit, their tape recorder broadcasting AC/DC's music to those below. They pass a road they are told leads to the garage where vehicles are fixed and gasoline purchased, and then they are among houses again. These are even more reminiscent of those in a Darwin suburb, as are the gardens of flowers, trees, and shrubs. Here is the outstation manager's house and there the carpenter's, and there is the house occupied by the charter plane pilot. Although there are a few Aboriginal families in this part of the settlement, most of the houses are occupied by whites. These are people like the electrician, plumber, accountant, mechanic, and town clerk, who have been hired by the Aboriginal Council, or the nurses, shop manager, and Bible translators who have come under the auspices of the mission society. School teachers hired by the Northern Territory's Department of Education also live in this area.

This is Mangrove, a community of approximately 420 Australian Aborigines and 45 whites, the home of Marguerite, Kay, and Nora.

THE ABORIGINES OF MANGROVE

Mangrove, first known as Sandy Creek Mission, was established in 1952 as a Protestant mission for the area's Aboriginal population.[1]

Until the mid-1960s when a mining town grew up about sixty miles away, Mangrove's closest neighbors were two other Aboriginal missions that had been established in the first half of the twentieth century, one about a hundred miles to the southwest of Mangrove, the other about fifty miles to the east. Together with a flying boat refueling station about eighty miles from Mangrove, these three missions were the only outposts of white culture for hundreds of miles.

Most of the grandparents of Mangrove's adolescents were, like all indigenous Australians, once nomadic hunters and gatherers; only a minority had spent most of their lives on one or another of the three mission settlements. Unlike their neighbors to the west and south whose countries had become permanent pastoral holdings in the late 1800s, the Aborigines of Mangrove did not, apparently, suffer from the same degree of ecological and social disruption associated elsewhere with the incursion of whites and cattle into Aboriginal territory.[2] Before settling, they exploited a costal strip of the area that extends north and south of the mission by about one hundred miles (Biernoff 1979, 153; Heath 1978, 12–14).

Informants speaking of nomadic times said they sometimes moved daily. Normally, however, during the "dry" part of the year, as many as two hundred people might be camped for at least three months on one site (Biernoff 1974, 273). But these were communities in flux. Groups as small as a single family consisting of a man, his wives, and children, or as large as twenty such families, might leave the larger community. These groups went on food-collecting expeditions or visited their own countries, sometimes for several months (pp. 275, 281–282). Seasonal flooding of the interior during the "wet" scattered the large inland communities. At this time of year, two or three families might camp together on the coast for as long as three months (Biernoff 1974, 274; see also White and Peterson 1969).

Material culture was simple; shelters, tools, and other objects were manufactured with relative ease from materials close at hand. Men fished and hunted for land animals and fowl. Dugong (a large herbivorous sea mammal) and sea turtle were harpooned when they came into the area to feed on local kelp beds. Women hunted smaller prey (e.g., goanna, a large lizard), fished, and gathered shellfish. They also collected vegetable foods such as water lily seeds and cycad nuts.

Aboriginal contact with whites and Western culture consisted primarily of contact with missions and mission personnel. It is not known when the Aborigines of Mangrove first began visiting the missions, but by the 1940s one of the three had become a regular stop on their annual trek (Cole 1982). There are no written accounts of the day-to-day lives of the Mangrove Aborigines prior to 1952 for no ethnographic work was undertaken during the presettlement period. That life on the settlement is associated with radical changes in Aboriginal existence is clear, however, from ethnographies of people in nearby areas at times when white presence had little disturbed Aboriginal social forms (Warner 1937; Rose 1960), from archeological reconstruction (Biernoff 1974), and from the statements of older informants who had spent their early years in the bush.

Adolescence at Mangrove in 1981 was largely an invention of settlement life, and so it is to the settlement that this introduction now turns.

THE SETTLEMENT

The settlement of Mangrove occupies a stretch of coastal land, beginning just a hundred yards or so inland from the high tide mark. The area it coveres is approximately one-quarter of a mile in width and one-half a mile in length.

In March of 1981, the Aboriginal residences of Mangrove included fifty-five houses, a tent, a trailer, and a "humpie" (a shack of boards and tin). Eighteen of the houses had been built since 1971. All but one of these newer houses were relatively large structures, approximately thirty feet by fifteen feet, containing several rooms, kitchen facilities, and plumbing. Most of the newer houses were raised about six feet above the ground. The remaining houses were much older. These were one- or two-room structures no larger than eight feet by fourteen feet. Some of these were raised off the ground by posts between two to six feet in height; others rested directly on the sand. None had plumbing. Their inhabitants used the public toilet and shower blocks, wash houses, and water taps spaced throughout the area. All of the houses were hooked up to electricity supplied by an oil-fed generator (see also Biernoff 1974, 279).

One of the larger houses sheltered widows and other unattached females. Three houses and a trailer sheltered the single men. Most of the remainder housed at least one married couple and their children. On the average, approximately seven people occupied each dwelling.[3] However, five houses were empty at the time of my residence survey and one housed twenty-five people.

Marguerite and Nora both lived with their families in the older sort of housing. Marguerite slept in one of the two rooms of her parents' house, sharing a room with her fourteen-year-old sister and her ten- and twelve-year-old brothers. The other room of the house sheltered her twenty-five-year-old sister, her sister's husband, and their three children—a six-year-old, a toddler, and an infant. Her twenty-two-year-old brother lived down the road in the trailer for single men. Recently, Marguerite's mother and father, Lily and Goodman, had moved to a one-room plank house not more than eight-feet square, just across the road from the house in which Marguerite slept. Here they slept with their youngest child, a girl of eight. Like most of Mangrove's Aboriginal residents, Marguerite and her family used their houses for little more than storage and sleeping (see also Biernoff 1979, 169). Their domestic domain consisted of the entire area between the two houses, including the narrow dirt road that separated them. Nearby trees, a cashew and a coconut palm planted at the time the mission was started, provided daytime protection from the heat and glare of the sun. The family cooked, ate, and rested in the shade of the houses and trees; the children played in the sand surrounding the buildings or in the red dirt of the road.

About 150 yards down the road was a house not unlike Lily's, only smaller and more decrepit, with broken wall boards and holes in the planks of the sagging porch. This was Nora's house. Nora slept in its one room, sharing her mattress with her baby daughter Leni, her mother Rosalind, and her ten-year-old brother. Her father, Guwagiyn, also known as Greenleaf, slept there as well on his own mattress. Nora's elder sister, and the sister's husband and two small children, lived in a similar house that faced Nora's across about twenty feet of sand. Across another twenty feet of sand to one side of Nora's house lived her thirty-year-old brother with his wife and two young sons. Her thirteen-year-old brother lived in the house of a clan brother of Rosalind's mother on the other side of the village.

Originally, Mangrove consisted of two residential neighborhoods that were separated from one another by the mission's church, the Aboriginal village, and what the Aborigines called the "missionarea." Once, only Aborigines lived in the village and only whites in the mission area. By 1981, however, four of the missionarea's twenty-one houses were occupied by Aboriginal families: one by the current council president, one by a past council president, and another by the only Aboriginal school-teacher on the settlement. The fourth had been given to Kay's mother's sister, thirty-five-year-old Majiwi. It had several rooms, electricity, and plumbing and was located just fifty yards or so from the new health clinic where Majiwi was a health worker. Kay lived with Majiwi. During 1981, after Kay's father died, Kay's mother, Bayarra, moved out of their family house in the village, as is appropriate when a death occurs. While Bayarra's house was uninhabitable due to the recent death, she, her mother, and two of her brother's children for whom she had been caring since their mother's death in 1978, moved in with Kay and Majiwi.[4] They slept in the bedroom with Majiwi; Kay had a bed to herself on the enclosed porch of the house.

Settlement living is clearly associated with demographic changes that are relevant to this description of adolescence. For example, Mangrove brings together a large number of adolescents, likely many more than were coresidents in pre-mission times. It is also possible that the settlement is associated with changes in the birth rate and rate of infant mortality, creating an adolescent age-group that is proportionately larger than it was in pre-mission times. In 1981, adolescent girls composed over 25 percent of the female population. The implications of these demographic shifts, particularly the development of an adolescent peer group, are discussed in chapter 4.

The settlement also provides diverse and unprecedented settings for adolescent interaction. One of the most important of these is the school.

THE SCHOOL

The school, begun in 1953 by the missionaries (Bayton 1965), was, in 1981, the domain of the Northern Territory's Department of Education. The nine school buildings occupied an area approximately the size of a large city block and included a separate preschool, home economics building, and manual arts hall. The staff was composed of ten teachers, one principal, and six Aboriginal teaching assistants. Enrollment was approximately

150 children between the ages of three and sixteen. By law, children between the ages of four and fourteen must attend school in Australia. Aboriginal children are accepted, however, at the age of three, and they, like their white counterparts, may remain in school after the legal age for leaving, which is fifteen. Mangrove's pupils attended school for three terms of twelve to fourteen weeks each in 1981. Class was held five days a week between 8:00 A.M. and 2:30 P.M. (8:30 to 3:00 in the cooler weather), with a half-hour recess and an hour for lunch. Preschool children attended during the morning session only, from 8:00 to 11:00.

The primary aim of the school was literacy and numeracy. Accordingly, reading, writing, mathematics, and English were taught at each level. Scripture was a part of the curriculum, as it is in any Australian public school. So was personal hygiene, at least for the postprimary girls, as a part of their health and physical education course. The youngest schoolchildren engaged in such activities as finger painting and singing, the older ones in arts and crafts, cooking, and sports. Extracurricular activities included school fetes and coeducational dances.

After preschool, children were placed in grades from one to five-six, largely on the basis of chronological age. At thirteen they moved to the postprimary class where they might stay until the age of seventeen. The postprimary curriculum included English, math, science, social science, health and physical education, and sports. Postprimary girls took home economics several days a week; boys took cooking one afternoon a week. The boys had technical studies (e.g., carpentry, metal work) several days a week; the girls had crafts two hours a week. All other classes in the postprimary grade were coeducational, as they were in the lower grades and at the preschool. Only in 1981 did the school begin to offer courses of study equivalent to those in high school programs elsewhere in Australia.

All instruction at the school from its inception was in English, though students might be addressed in the Aboriginal language by the teaching assistants. A program in bilingual education was started around 1975, but as none of the white teachers spoke the Aboriginal language, nor was it clear that their students did either, preferring to speak Kriol when they were not speaking Aboriginal English, it was discontinued at the end of 1978.

Nora, Marguerite, and Kay had all attended Mangrove's school, but not for some time prior to this study. Marguerite had stayed in school until she was seventeen, Kay had left at fifteen, and Nora had left when she was fourteen. None had graduated, of course, for there was no program to graduate from until 1981. Kay had, however, received further training at Batchelor, an Aboriginal college outside of Darwin, in order to qualify as a teaching assistant. School personnel had also suggested that Marguerite might go to Batchelor to be trained as a teaching assistant in the preschool, but she had not wanted to go. As far as Lily, her mother, was concerned, Batchelor was a place where Aboriginal girls made "friend" with men who took them to far away places or left them with a "single baby."

Of the three, only Kay was clearly using the skills she had learned at school. But the school at Mangrove taught adolescents more than just skills. The school inculcated Aboriginal children with many of the values, beliefs, and expectations of the dominant society. The missionaries instructed them in schedules and scriptures and taught them to brush their teeth, to excuse themselves when they belched, to garden, chop wood, and wash clothes and dishes. The Department of Education teachers continued some of these lessons, teaching their pupils such things as proper classroom comportment and the Western versions of punctuality, grooming, and cleanliness.

It has also been largely through the school that the Aboriginal children of Mangrove have been exposed to many of the products and entertainments of the Western world, from books, magazines, paper and crayons, to stoves, washing machines, and carpenter's tools. By 1981, the school's inventory included a piano, skate boards, a trampoline, and a video-cassette machine.

The school has also provided some examples of white behavior unlike that of the missionaries'. Through the school, Aboriginal children have become acquainted with whites who are not "Christians," who drink alcohol, wear eye shadow and sarongs, and play rock, jazz, and disco music on their stereos.

Perhaps of equal significance, schooling likely means that Aboriginal children have not learned some of the things they would have in earlier times. In other settings, Aboriginal children are rarely, if ever, instructed; they learn primarily through contact with and observation of other people (Harris 1980, 21).

But from 1953 onward, the school at Mangrove has removed the children from the vicinity of Aboriginal adults for a good part of the day. Thus their opportunities to learn from Aboriginal people are curtailed, and some of what was once learned by Aboriginal children has probably been missed by the Western-educated young of the settlement. For example, in other times, when adolescents like Marguerite, Kay, and Nora were little girls, they would have accompanied their mothers and grandmothers on many of their near-daily gathering expeditions. Playing nearby the group of gathering women, they would have watched and learned the techniques employed in the pursuit of particular foodstuffs, the location of various plant and animal foods, and the time of year when they were to be found in specific locations—perhaps one of the most essential kinds of knowledge needed by Australian food gatherers. For the school-girl, confined to the classroom five days a week, for nine months of the year, these opportunities are limited to weekends and holidays.

Aboriginal children on the settlement are not entirely cut off from their cultural heritage, however. They still spend many hours a day in the village, where their parents and other adults are nearby. They listen to the stories of the old people and likely overhear a great deal of adult conversation, learning not only current human events, for such are the invariable topics of conversation, but also the beliefs, values, and expectations that are inevitably expressed in these discussions. Little girls spend enough time by their mothers' sides to have learned by the age of ten or eleven how to build and light a fire, boil a billy of tea, and cook damper, the white-flour bread that is a staple of today's diet. They learn to fish with lines as their mothers cast into the nearby river channel, and at least some may learn how and where to collect the once-staple water lily seed and hunt for goanna, though in these pursuits they are more likely taught by their grandmothers than by their mothers. Similarly, boys learn to handle the trident fish spears wielded by men in the shallow waters of the bay. On weekend trips into the bush, now made by Land Rover and Toyota, they learn to track and shoot, and a few, accompanying their elders, now in motorized boats rather than dugout canoes, learn to harpoon the large sea turtles and dugong that are still an important source of protein for the people of the settlement. Both boys and girls also learn at least some aspects of the indigenous system of social organization.

Throughout the formative years, the adolescents of Mangrove have been exposed to the teachings of two divergent cultures: the Western culture of school and church and the Aboriginal culture, albeit already modified by Western elements, of their parents and grandparents. There is little doubt that these daily experiences of school and village, so often divorced from one another, contribute to the conflict between generations. This theme as it is manifest in conflicts over sex and marriage is explored further in chapters 3 and 4.

SUBSISTENCE

In 1981 Mangrove was basically a service economy supported by government funds. Men and women worked as teaching assistants in the school or as clerks in the shop and office. Men worked in the workshop and garage and on the work crews that graded the dirt roads and did rough carpentry and other maintenance labor. Women worked as cleaners for the shop, office, clinic, community toilets, and church. Majiwi, Kay's mother's sister, and another woman were trained as health workers, two others as a schoolteacher and a community welfare worker. One man was trained as a police aid.

In 1981 Mangrove was funded by the Northern Territory's Department of Community Development, the Department of Aboriginal Affairs, and the Aboriginal Development Commission. Laborers received the Australian minimum wage of $4.40 per hour, earning $154 for the thirty-five-hour work week. Work team supervisors received $5.20 per hour. Aborigines working in positions once occupied by whites earned more. For example, the salary of the assistant town clerk was $13,000 per year. (All dollar amounts are Australian dollars, worth about 1.2 American dollars in 1981.)

Unlike Kay, young people did not as a rule move into the work force upon leaving school. In 1981 approximately nineteen boys and twenty-four girls were between the ages of fourteen and seventeen on the settlement. Of these, at least eight boys and seven girls had left school by the middle of the school year. But most of them had not moved into jobs. Although fifteen is the legal minimum age for employment in Australia, only one boy, a seventeen-year-old, and two girls besides Kay, one aged sixteen and one aged eighteen, were working by June of 1981.

For girls, this employment picture is unlikely to change in the near future if the example of their elders is any indication of career patterns. Of the sixteen females employed at Mangrove in May and June of 1981, only two were in their midtwenties. Except for the three teenagers, the other female workers were all at least thirty years of age. It is possible that the women of Mangrove do not generally work during their teens and twenties because they are bearing and raising children during these years.

For at least some of the unemployed boys, jobs might come a bit earlier. Males between the ages of eighteen and twenty-nine made up 67 percent of the male work force in May and June of 1981. These workers, however, comprised only 39 percent of their age-sex group on the settlement.

Employment, particularly in Western-type occupations, has always been limited at Mangrove.[5] Taking the potential work force to be all males and females between the ages of fifteen and fifty-nine, approximately 13 percent of the female work force and 23 percent of the male work force were employed in May and June of 1981.[6]

Limited job opportunities are probably not the whole story of low employment at Mangrove. In 1981, for example, when there was a high rate of unemployment, there were also unfilled job openings on seven of the eight work teams and a position at the clinic that remained vacant for months. There were also twenty-one positions at Mangrove in that year, not including those of the minister or Bible translators, filled by whites. These jobs included bank clerk, plumber, mechanic, nurse, schoolteacher, shop manager, and accountant, for which most of the local people had little or no training.

The unemployment of Nora and Marguerite is much more characteristic of Mangrove's adolescent population than Kay's employed status. Like others in their situation, Marguerite and Nora were welfare recipients. According to the guide to Social Security benefits, Marguerite received unemployment compensation of $106.90 every fortnight. Nora as a single mother of one child received a fortnightly check of about $165. In 1981 the Aborigines of Mangrove were receiving some of the benefits and services they were entitled to as Australian citizens. For example, women over sixty, men over sixty-five, and invalids received government pensions. Women like Nora with dependent children to support on their own received Supporting Parents Benefits. Unemployment benefits were regularly distributed to unemployed people over the age of sixteen. If recipients were offered jobs and refused them, and if this was reported to the Department of Social Security in Darwin, they would be struck off the rolls. Reapplication was a process that took about six weeks. A breakdown of such income was not available, but in the month of March 1981 the town clerk estimated that about $16,000 worth of pension and unemployment checks were cashed each fortnight. This amounts to about $38 per person every two weeks.

The Aborigines of Mangrove in 1981 appeared to rely heavily on the Western foods purchased in the shop, for example, flour, tea, sugar, and frozen and canned meat and vegetables. In the households with which I was familiar, a staple of the diet was damper (bread). A number of women were observed hunting, fishing, and gathering near the settlement on one occasion or another. However, the women observed going out into the bush with some regularity were usually between fifty and sixty years of age. Men also continued to hunt and fish, though not, presumably, to the same extent as they did before their involvement in wage labor. Although the hunters appeared to be a younger group than the gatherers, their numbers did not include the teenage males. The unemployed young did not generally appear to spend their time in alternate economic pursuits. They were rarely observed in any sort of hunting and gathering activity. And unlike a number of the older men and women who earned some cash by making and selling such objects as bark paintings and pandanus baskets, none of the adolescents produced handicrafts.

Work of any sort did not appear to be a necessity for the adolescents of Mangrove. Subsistence depended neither on their skills as hunters and gatherers nor on the Western schooling that they had received. Consequently, few demands were placed on the time and energy of the adolescents, especially those who were out of school, unemployed, and unmarried.

THE DAILY ROUTINE OF ADOLESCENTS

Mangrove is close to the equator and so the sun was always well into the sky when the church bell rang each morning at 7:30 A.M. during the year of 1981.[7] Adolescents like Kay who had jobs to start or school to attend might well be up and eating breakfast by this time, for work and school began at 8:00. The first meal of the day generally consisted of damper and tea—black and heavily sugared. According to Kay, she cooked breakfast for her family before leaving for work. Marguerite and Nora were more likely to eat food prepared by their mothers. Nora had her baby daughter to care for from the time they both awoke, but Marguerite had few demands placed upon her time. Following a late night at cards or some other recreation, she might sleep later than the rest of the family and breakfast after the school children had departed.

By 8:00 Kay was at school, meeting with the second-grade teacher whom she was assisting that year. If Marguerite were awake by this time, she was likely to be sitting under the shade of the cashew tree with a cup of tea and a piece of damper in her hands, watching her mother, Lily, stitch on a pandanus basket and listening to the conversation of the inevitable stream of neighbors and kinsmen who stopped to visit. Similarly, Nora was likely to spend the early part of the morning by her mother's side, listening to the conversation between Rosalind and her various visitors. She would breast-feed Leni and hold her in her lap when the baby girl was not toddling about in the sand around the breakfast fire.

Ten o'clock was *smoko* or "morning tea time." The school-children were given a half-hour recess and workers a fifteen-minute break. At this time the shop became a busy place as children came to buy a morning soft drink and bag of chips. The work crews would gather on the lawn near the office in white or black cliques. Women would walk up from the village to meet with their female friends, kinswomen, and children out of school. The old men would sit in groups by the outdoor movie screen or in the shade of the council hall; the women would gather in the sandy yard in front of the shop. Marguerite, Kay, and Nora would all be likely to visit the shop at this hour. There they might buy a cold drink or a pack of cigarettes and meet with the other adolescents who had gathered there.

After the morning tea break, Nora's mother, Rosalind, would often collect a billy can and water, tea, sugar, the makings of damper, and a bed sheet or two, and walk down to the beach. There she and her husband, Greenleaf, would spend the rest of the day sitting in the shade of the coconut trees. If the tide was right they might go fishing after the sun passed its peak, but otherwise they moved only to keep in the shade cast by the trees. Nora would usually accompany her mother, as might her ten-year-old brother—who was often truant from school—her elder sister and two children, and her elder brother's three-year-old son. There in the sand, Nora would nurse and play with Leni, sleep, eat lunch, talk, and quarrel with the other family members until the sun began to set and they all returned to their little house in the village. On days that the mail was brought from Darwin, Nora might go up to the office to watch the mail come in and see if her welfare check had come. Or if she had some money she might leave Leni with Rosalind and find a card game.

Marguerite spent her mornings in various ways. Sometimes she would stay around the family area, rarely helping Lily by fetching something or her elder sister by caring for one of her young children. More often she would sit in the shade, smoke, comb her hair, or talk to a visitor. Other times she would walk around the settlement, sometimes with a female peer, sometimes alone. She might visit various friends and kin or she might visit the anthropologist. Like Nora, when she had money she might find a card game to join.

At noon Kay would leave the school and walk the short distance to her house, where she would eat lunch with her family. Having eaten, she often joined her next-door neighbors and close kinswomen, two unmarried half-sisters, aged twenty-three and thirty-two. The three young women might play tapes on their cassette recorder, smoke, and delouse each others' hair for what remained of Kay's lunch hour.

After the lunch break when the schoolchildren had returned to school, the village took on a deserted aspect. Here and there one might see a reclining figure in the shade of a tree or a few very small children playing in the sand. Even the dogs would sleep during the hot afternoon hours. An occasional council vehicle might rumble along the road, and the ever-present crows would cackle and caw as they raided the trash barrels. Otherwise the village was silent. A nap, a card game, or a conversation might occupy Nora or Marguerite during this time of day. If the second graders spent the afternoon in the library watching the video, Kay might stay alone in the classroom doing paper work or writing in her diary. Or she might walk across the school yard to chat with the Aboriginal schoolteacher who was her neighbor and close kinswoman. After school she sometimes joined Majiwi, the clinic cleaning women, and visiting women like her mother in their conversation on the clinic veranda.

The schoolchildren were dismissed at 2:30 or 3:00 and shortly after that some of the work teams began to "knock off," though the clinic, shop, and office remained open until 5:00. As the heat of the day abated, people were again seen in the yards and roads of the village. The shop and office areas became busy once more as schoolchildren and workers sought another cold soft drink and women shopped for dinner. Children played in the road and the sand around the houses. Hunters and gatherers returned from the ocean or bush. As fires were lit in the yards and women began their preparations for the evening meal, people would drift back to the village and cluster around these hearths.

At this time of day many of the adolescents of Mangrove could be found at the basketball court, in the yard of the now-closed school, on the platforms of the water tower, or around the deserted office and shop area. The basketball court in particular was a place where adolescents gathered as the sun began to set. Located several hundred yards from the edge of the village and surrounded by tall grass and trees, it was a relatively private place, especially when compared to the village, where the view over expansive white sand hills was impeded only by houses and an occasional tree. The postprimary children were taken there frequently by their teachers for their afternoon sports.

Then, when the teachers left, the children were joined in their game by older adolescents and those who had left school.

During this time of day, Kay, now off work, would meet one or another of her female friends, like her "best friend," Marylou, who worked as a clerk in the shop. The two teenagers might listen to the music on their cassettes (Elvis Presley was one favorite), smoke, talk about boys, and share a shower. Nora was more likely to be with her mother, accompanying her on her evening quest for firewood or mixing up the evening batch of damper.

After dark, adolescents who were not at home sitting around the supper fires with the rest of their families might be at the school watching the video or a movie, playing cards in one of the village games, or going off to the beach or to one of the nearby sandhills on a "date" (see chap. 4), or sniffing petrol.[8] As one of the adolescents who sometimes engaged in the latter activity, Marguerite might spend an evening with a group of adolescent boys and girls, holding their soft drink cans filled with gasoline and inhaling the fumes.

THE LAW: SOCIAL ORGANIZATION AND RELIGION

The social identity of the Aborigines of Mangrove rests, in large part, on a series of statuses clearly derived from the indigenous system of social organization, however that might have been changed by the mission situation. These statuses, which are expressed as kin classifications and as "country," clan, and moiety affiliations, are assigned on the basis of culturally recognized connections between a woman and her child and a man and his child. Sections and subsections are not social categories usually employed at Mangrove (Capell 1960, 31; Shapiro 1977, 40).

At the core of Aboriginal social identity is the relationship of the individual to his or her "country." When the people of Mangrove were nomads, movement between territories was not normally curtailed. Stretches of territory were regarded, however, as belonging to specific groups of people. At the centers of these territories are billabongs (ponds), or sections of a river or stream. These localities are associated with the "Dreaming" (which will be discussed in a moment) and are regarded as sacred. It is in these waters that the people of a "country" reside before they are born and after they die. Conversely, it is people from these waters who are regarded as the "owners" of the territory that surrounds a specific sacred site. As a general rule, a child is said to come from his father's country, and so shares his country group, clan, and moiety.[9] Country groups, clans, and moieties are associated with rules of exogamy; according to the Law (discussed below), a man should not marry a woman who shares either his country, clan, or moiety. A child also has an important relationship to his mother's country, called his "milk country." He or she is regarded as its "manager," particularly of its sacred area and associated rituals (see also Biernoff 1979, 153–154; Capell 1960, 31–32; Heath 1980, 5–6; Hughes 1971, i–iv; van der Leeden 1975).

The Aboriginal people at Mangrove address and refer to each other with a series of kin terms. These terms are extended to all known individuals, not just genealogical relatives. Each of these terms is associated with a child term. That is, individuals are addressed or referred to by specific terms because one of their parents is referred to by the associated term. An informant might say, for example, "I call her father's sister because I call her mother father's mother." Both male and female terms are associated with child terms. Ideally, a person would call each member of a couple by terms associated with the same child term. Sometimes, however, a person calls each member of a couple by terms associated with different child terms. When this occurs, as it does in the case of an incorrect marriage (chap. 3), a choice must be made between the two associated child terms. For example, an individual might call the father of a child "brother" and the mother of a child "mother." He would then have to decide if it would be best to call the child "brother's child" or "sibling" (see also Shapiro 1981, 34–35). This decision appears to rest on whether a person regards the child's mother or father as his or her closest relative (Burbank 1980, 32–35; see also Turner 1974, 58). Because the statuses associated with at least some of these terms set parameters for social interaction, it is necessary for the individual to know what he calls the people around him and what they in turn call him. For example, rules of etiquette require that women know whom they call "brother" and "son-in-law" (see Burbank 1980, 165–175, 209–212; 1985). In chapters 4 and 5 I discuss how the incorrect marriages made by today's adolescents may have the potential for disrupting the system of kin classification currently employed at Mangrove.

The Dreaming is a time both past and present. In the past, the Dreaming was a time when aspects of the natural and social worlds of the Australian Aborigine were created. In the present, it is a charter of what may and should be, a codification of the moral system (Stanner 1965). When the Aborigines of Mangrove speak of the Dreaming, or the Law, they use the phrases to explain such things as features in the natural environment, the way that a ceremony is to be performed, the expected form of interpersonal relations, and the ideal marriage system.

The Law is presented in three ceremonies that are held at Mangrove, including the male circumcision ceremony. In each of these there are sacred components that are kept from all but those who have been initiated into their secrets. But each ceremony also has public components that can be witnessed by women and uninitiated males. In each of these ceremonies the world as it is and should be, the world as it was created in the Dreaming, is presented by the dance, song, and painted bodies of the performers. Each of the ceremonies has an initiatory component as well, and males are gradually initiated into the sacred world (see also Heath 1980; Hughes 1971, v).

THE YOUNG BOYS OF MANGROVE

If it were not for the participation of young boys, the sexual behavior of young girls that so disturbs many adults of Mangrove would not be possible. For the reasons stated in chapter 1, my understanding of these young boys is limited. Nevertheless, since they are an important part of the social setting for adolescent girls, a rough sketch of at least some aspects of their life on the settlement is in order.

A boy at Mangrove becomes a young boy as his body approaches adult size, his facial hair becomes visible, and his voice begins to deepen. By fourteen years of age, most of Mangrove's males are regarded as young boys. Marriage and the birth of children bring an end to this stage, and a young boy becomes a "man." In 1981 the median age at marriage for the males of the settlement was twenty-two-and-a-half, and within a year or two of their marriages many had become fathers.[10]

A number of factors suggest the extent to which today's median male marriage age represents a change from the past. First, according to the logic of the ideal marriage system (detailed in the next chapter), a firstborn male in pre-mission times could not expect to marry until he was in his late twenties or early thirties. (By marriage I mean actually living with a spouse. I discuss this point further in chap. 4. See also Shapiro 1979, 83–85ff.). Younger sons could expect to marry even later, for, according to the ideal, their legitimate wives were the widows of their elder brothers. Several older women said that in past times it was the Law to marry "old men," that is, men with long beards or some gray in their hair. In 1981 the age at which some of the settlement's males were marrying elicited the scorn of at least one older woman. She, for example, ridiculed a recent groom of twenty-three who was, from her perspective, too young to marry. According to Rose, before missionaries had made much headway on Groote Eylandt, women were monopolized by men over the age of thirty. None of the men between the ages of sixteen and twenty in his sample had wives, and less than half of those between twenty-one and thirty were married (Rose 1960, 91, 69). According to Webb, a missionary working with the Murngin in the late 1920s, twenty-five was the earliest age that a man might have a wife (Rose 1960, 93). Thus, it seems likely that in earlier times many, if not most, of the Aboriginal males of the Mangrove area remained bachelors until late in their twenties.

In 1981 approximately seventy-five males between fourteen and twenty-nine were living on the settlement.[11] Of these, twenty-six were married and another three divorced. All but one of the married men (or once-married men) were between the ages of twenty and twenty-nine, accounting for approximately 61 percent of this age-group. Eighteen of the married men were fathers; the wives of two others were pregnant with their first child.

The period of maidenhood has lengthened, if not actually come into existence, for the female adolescents of Mangrove. The period of bachelorhood, on the other hand, a major characteristic of Aboriginal male adolescence, appears now to be shorter, at least for some in the male population. But more than the length of this life stage may have changed for the young boys of the settlement. Today when young girls choose a man to marry, they may be choosing a male who is not only chronologically younger than husbands generally were in the past, but also one who is less socially mature according to Aboriginal standards.

THE SOCIAL CONTROL OF MALE ADOLESCENTS

The sexual behavior of young unmarried males has, it appears, often, if not always, been a problem in Aboriginal Australia. According to Frederick Rose, the "dilemma" of Aboriginal societies is this: older polygynists monopolize the women, leaving young men, at the "peak" of their physical and sexual powers, "virtually without women" (Rose 1968, 207). The solution to this dilemma, says Rose, is the elaborate system of male initiation, which engages the youth from before puberty through his mid to late twenties, for until he completes his initiation he cannot marry (Rose 1968, 207; see also Bern 1979; Hiatt 1985; Keen 1982, 621).

In fact, while older males may have delayed marriage for younger men through their control of ritual, initiation does not appear to have prevented all forms of sexual behavior for the young male (Shapiro 1979, 86). For example, the reputation of young men as adulterers was widespread (see, for example, Meggitt 1962, 234; Hiatt 1965, 107). Even marriage itself may not have been much delayed for the young man willing to risk the consequences of eloping with another man's wife or stealing a woman from another group (Worsley 1954, in Rose 1960, 74; Warner 1969, 71). The issue at hand, however, is not that the young men of Mangrove are adulterers (though they sometimes are) but rather that some of these young men marry young women who are not correct marriage partners and that the sexual behavior of the young often precipitates these incorrect marriages.

A number of Australian ethnographers have noted the tolerance with which Aborigines treat adultery (see, for example, Hiatt 1965, 105–112; Worsley 1954, 218, quoted in Rose 1960, 74). Most recently, Francesca Merlan has explored the congruence of this attitude with an "ideological disjunction between sexuality and marriage" (Merlan n.d., 1986). Adultery, however, may be the first step toward the marriage of a man and a woman who has been betrothed, if not actually living with another (Shapiro 1981, 70–71; see also Warner 1937, 73). It is the stealing of a woman and the breaking up of a marriage that are regarded as "serious matters" (Worsley 1954, 217, quoted in Rose 1960, 74).

There have always been Aborigines who did not marry correctly, even in traditional times. However, as I detail in chapter 3, evidence suggests that incorrect unions at Mangrove are on the rise. It also appears that the extent to which the young are ignoring the rules for establishing unions is without precedent.

While regulating the behavior of young males has long been a task for Aboriginal society, at Mangrove the task may currently be more difficult due to changes in three related domains of Aboriginal life: the residence of bachelors, the manner and content of male education, and limitations of the Law on the settlement (see also Hiatt 1985, 44; Wallace 1977, 87).

THE BACHELORS' CAMP

In 1981 some of the young boys at Mangrove lived in three houses and a house trailer. One of these residences was about a quarter of a mile from the Aboriginal village. The others were located within the Aboriginal village and were in no way segregated from the households of single women or married couples and their children. These "single quarters" are the settlement version of the bachelors' camp of pre-mission times. These were sometimes located away from the households of married men by as much as a half a mile (see also Biernoff 1974, 277). W. L. Warner described the "men's camp" of the Murngin as one inhabited by boys from the age of their circumcision (between six and eight years of age) until they married. It was also the residence of male visitors traveling without their wives (Warner 1969, 116–117).

According to Warner's informants, a major feature of the camp was sexual segregation: "when a boy gets older he sees [his parents engage in sexual intercourse], and then he says,

"That's good for me, too." He goes and gets a young girl . . . and they go into the bush. When he stays in the big camp he sees too many women" (Warner 1969, 116). Older informants at Mangrove also said that in the past, unmarried men were expected to stay away from their brothers' wives; at least two mentioned cases of married men throwing spears at bachelors who had approached their womenfolk.

Sexual segregation is clearly one means of controlling heterosexual activity. Today's presence of unmarried males in the midst of sexually mature females is an aspect of Mangrove's social organization with clear implications for the problem of adolescent sexuality.

THE EDUCATION OF YOUNG BOYS

According to Warner, the older residents of Murngin men's camps taught younger members the etiquette and ritual knowledge appropriate for their age and sex (Warner 1969, 116–117). Education was also an aspect of camp life for unmarried males on Groote Eylandt. During his years in the bachelors' camp, a boy was instructed in hunting and "the other manly arts" (Rose 1968, 207). According to Tindale (who spent fifteen months in the Groote Eylandt area in 1921 and 1922), a boy lived in the men's camp under the guardianship of an older man from the time of his circumcision until the age of about seventeen (Tindale 1925–1926, 1, 67–68).[12] Rose describes this guardian as the prospective husband of the boy's sister (Rose 1960, 221). During his years in camp, a boy did such chores as collecting firewood and hauling water. He also performed personal services for his guardian: "One such guardian, . . . had two boys under his care; they were never allowed out of his sight, followed him when hunting, and when in camp attended frequently to his person, combing his hair, removing lice therefrom, and sometimes red ochreing his body all over" (Tindale 1925–1926, 68). The guardianship "lapsed" after the boy received his first chest cut. Males in the area of Mangrove were scarified in this way (p. 69). It is not clear, however, if they were also initiates of their sisters' husbands like the Groote Eylandt boys.

Since the mission at Mangrove began (and health clinic records have been kept), boys have usually been circumcised between the ages of eight and eleven. A boy, by the act of having his foreskin removed, is made a "young man," but is still regarded as a "little boy." He will not become a "young boy" for several years to come, and few, if any, changes are expected in his behavior. He remains living with his family of orientation until he is in his midteens. Then he may move to one or another of the single quarters, move into a friend's or relative's house, or continue living at home.

It is not at the age of circumcision, but in the midteens, when boys are regarded as young boys, that they are thought to have enough "sense" to at least begin to learn the proper adult behavior that is the mark of a man. The extent to which the young boys at Mangrove today are learning what they were once expected to learn is not clear, however. It may be that many of the situations for learning about male ritual and etiquette no longer exist (see also Bell and Ditton 1980, 27).

For example, it is a commonplace of today's settlement that much of the ritual knowledge has not been passed on to the younger generations; their elders have judged them lacking in the prerequisite qualities for indoctrination in the Law. There are also suggestions that some of the young males are not participating in the rituals that once would have initiated them into the world of the adult male.

A person who witnesses a ceremony is expected to behave properly and follow the Law. In particular, an initiate should not steal another man's wife or betrothed, fight, or cause any sort of trouble. In the past, I was told, a young boy who misbehaved after taking part in a ceremony would have been speared and killed, but in 1981, fear of the "white law" prevented such punishment. Instead, misbehavior was said to be punished with sorcery; unlike spears, sorcery can hit not only the culprit, but also any member of his kindred (see also Biernoff 1982).

According to one of my male informants, until a man has a long beard and is clearly knowledgeable and well behaved, whether or not he attends a ceremony is not his decision. This rests with his mother and her sisters and brothers.[13] They, perhaps in consultation with their mother and father and the boy's father, decide whether or not a boy's "character and behavior" are such that he might attend. Today it may be that some young men are judged ineligible. This judgment is, perhaps, from his kindred's point of view, less of a risk; the mundane consequences of misbehavior are less fearsome than those that are associated with the sacred domain.

In addition, contemporary cermonies at Mangrove appear to have lost components that were once of educational importance. One of these was a period of time when the initiate was taken to visit nearby language groups to invite them to his circumcision. A second was the period of seclusion following the operation (see also Heath 1980, 275). According to Warner's account of Murngin circumcision, the latter period was characterized by ritual instruction and the teaching of correct behavior (Warner 1969, 278). Similarly, in Mangrove's past, participation in the ceremony that followed circumcision in the cycle included a period of seclusion that might last for two months. According to one informant, this seclusion now lasts for only a week. In addition, because many of the young boys no longer live in the single quarters with older bachelors and widowers, they no longer have an opportunity to learn what their seniors might have once taught them in the context of the bachelors' camp.

Another aspect of this issue may be the extent to which the younger generation is not interested in ritual knowledge and Aboriginal etiquette, given that generation's assimilation into a larger world that is often ignorant or scornful of such behavior. Fred Myers has suggested that once, through the long ordeal of initiation, "rebellious young males internalized and came to identify with important aspects of the Law, eventually taking on responsibility for its enactment and transmission" (Myers 1980b, 212). But as both he (Myers 1980b, 211–212) and Sackett (1978, 116) point out, such a process may depend on intellectual isolation: the initiate must know of no alternative (see also Hiatt 1985, 44). Today at Mangrove, however, the Law must compete with the lessons of school, church, movies, and Western music. Initiation may no longer be viewed by the initiate himself as a means to a desired end—the achievement of adult male status. Rather, it may be seen as a nonsensical ordeal of pain and privation (Sackett 1978, 121–122; Wallace 1977; 81). Under these circumstances, its ability to affect subsequent behavior may be minimized.

LIMITS OF THE LAW

It can only be assumed that prior to settlement the people of Mangrove, like other indigenous Australians, had "no formal apparatus of government, no enduring hierarchy of authority," and "no recognized political leaders" (Meggitt 1966, 74). The political order was not a thing apart from the religious, moral, or domestic order (Meggitt 1966; Hiatt 1965; Myers 1980a, 1980b). If the Aborigines of Mangrove were like others on the continent, they obeyed their Law or suffered the consequences, but they did not, by and large, obey other humans. They were punished for transgressions, conceivably with death for serious offenses, but by an authority that was only the transient condition of those with knowledge of the Law (Myers 1979, 1980a, 1980b). On a day-to-day basis, communal life was maintained by the common values, shared experience, and shared expectations of the community (Hiatt 1965, 146–147). The inevitable clash of human wills and interests might be dealt with by contenders and supporters more on the basis of personal interests and relationships than on abstract conceptions of right and wrong (Berndt 1965a, 201–203; cf. Hiatt 1965, 146–147).

Presumably, permanent residence on the mission brought great changes in authority and law. According to a missionary present in the early mission days, the Aborigines of Sandy Creek Mission were "wards" of the state under the "care, charge and control" of the mission authorities. The missionaries at Mangrove in its first decade were, in a sense, an arm of the Australian government. Funded by the Commonwealth, they were encouraged to ensure that their charges stayed within the law of the dominant society. Aboriginal social life could exist only as long as it did not "fall afoul of the Commonwealth's standards of life." What were regarded as serious breaches of Australian law could be punished with expulsion from the mission. For lesser offenses, Aborigines were denied work, given extra work for no pay, or banned from the shop. In cases of murder, manslaughter, injurious assault, and in some cases of theft, the police, stationed in towns miles away from the settlement, were called to remove the offenders. The prisoners would be tried in a court of white Australia and, if found guilty, imprisoned in such places as Darwin's Fanny Bay Jail.

Judging from entries in the mission's journals, the arm of the missionaries reached into nearly every domain of the Aborigines' daily life. In addition to controlling much of the activity, education, diet, and personal hygiene of the children and the economic life of adults, the missionaries also attempted to control what were, certainly from the Aboriginal perspective, largely domestic matters. They attempted to control the movement and location of people, their housekeeping, their recreation, and their comportment. They also attempted to control actions that were, from the Aboriginal perspective, legitimate means of reacting to breaches of their own etiquette and law. For example, Aboriginal people punishing lawbreakers with physical violence were censored and fined by the missionaries.

In the 1960s, however, when the legal and civil status of Australian Aborigines began to change, the authority of the missionaries began to wane. The first sign of the change was, perhaps, the establishment of a station council, which was formed by the missionaries but included a number of Aboriginal representatives (Cole 1982, 48). The role of mission superintendent evolved into that of community adviser, a position discontinued in 1978. In that year, the mission turned over the management of Mangrove to the all-Aboriginal council.

By 1981 Mangrove's station council had become a town council. It consisted of two male representatives from each of the ten resident clans. The town clerk, a white employee of the council, attended meetings but only in an advisory capacity. The council received and distributed all government money coming to the settlement. It was, consequently, the major employer of both white and Aboriginal workers. The council had the right to make and enforce settlement rules and the responsibility for maintaining community order. It was the council that called in the police, when needed.

As the population of Mangrove has increased, so have breaches of the peace. Some disturbances, such as fights, have always occurred on the settlement. But in recent years, new forms of behavior that disrupt community life and violate white-imposed, if not Aboriginal, standards have made their appearance. Gambling, drinking alcohol, and petrol sniffing have all made their appearance on the settlement. Young people have begun to vandalize school property, scribble graffiti on community building walls, and take council vehicles for what can only be described as joyrides.

What is significant for this description of adolescence at Mangrove is that a considerable proportion of these new and disruptive behaviors appear to be innovations of the young, particularly males. Gambling attracts male and female, young and old alike. Alcohol intoxication, however, seems to be the province of males in their twenties. Only a handful of older men and a few younger boys were reported to drink. Similarly, petrol sniffing was first reported among the young men. Break-ins, vandalism, and illegal use of vehicles also appear to be largely the doing of male adolescents.

Adolescent girls also contribute to community disruption. Their sexual behavior has caused considerable concern and disruption, as will be seen in chapter 4. By 1981 some of the young girls had also joined the boys who sniffed petrol and broke into or vandalized buildings.

Before the introduction of Western goods, the Aborigines lived with only the tools and objects of a simple material culture. Most of these could be given away willingly or abandoned with little regret when a group moved on. There was, consequently, little need and little opportunity for crimes against property; there were no vehicles to steal nor buildings to vandalize. Similarly, the Aborigines never gathered or manufactured intoxicants. Though they may have occasionally obtained alcohol from the Macassans who camped in the area prior to white contact (Turner 1974, 179–180), the alcohol and petrol intoxication that is associated with some of the settlement's lawbreaking is largely without precedent in Aboriginal experience. In the past, wives could be "stolen," and people could, and likely did, aggress upon others or make demands that were not always reasonable or just. But these were largely personal matters to be dealt with on the spot by the offended parties and their more immediate kin. When, on the other hand, several young boys break into the shop and take goods from it, they offend no one in the Aboriginal community directly, nor have they broken the Law.

By 1981, white-imposed laws and authority had clearly undermined a primary form of Aboriginal social control at Mangrove—the threat of aggressive retaliation for wrongdoing. It also appears that contemporary experience had undermined the moral authority of the Law. But it is unclear to what extent white laws and white forms of authority, though adopted by the official Aboriginal body of the community, are regarded as legitimate by the Aboriginal community. It is unclear that white law has replaced the Law (see also Myers 1980a).

THE OUTSTATIONS

Beginning in 1977, people who had lived on the settlement for years began to move away from Mangrove. Permanent and semipermanent dwellings were set up in eleven small communities called outstations, on the territories associated with the various country groups (see also Young 1980; for a discussion of the outstation movement see Coombs, Dexter, and Hiatt 1980). The station farthest from Mangrove is located approximately sixty miles northwest from the settlement.

For at least some of the outstation residents, their move away from the settlement was seen as means of regaining their autonomy and preserving their traditions and Law. Though they still relied on some provisions from the shop, people on the stations hunted, fished, and gathered to a greater extent than they did on the settlement. Traditional forms of singing and dancing provided evening amusement on the largest of the outstations. In 1981 this outstation also hosted one of the three Law ceremonies mentioned earlier in this chapter. On other stations, people simply pursued their hunting and gathering and other activites in the absence of a white-imposed infrastructure of jobs and schedules.

The outstations are linked to Mangrove by unpaved roads and tracks that become impassable by vehicle in the wet season. In 1981 two of the outstations were maintained year round. At first, inhabitants of the other outstations had appeared to be setting a pattern of dual residence: the rainy season was spent on the settlement, the dry spent in the bush. In 1978 approximately half of Mangrove's adult population had houses or relatively permanent shelters on one or another of the outstations and spent at least a month out of the year away from Mangrove. In 1981, however, people appeared to be spending less time on the outstations. Two had no residents during the nine months of my second field trip, and several others were visited only on weekends by many of their previous residents.

Even in the context of diminished adult participation, adolescents were noticeably absent from the outstations. At most, only one or two were present on the five outstations that I visited, and as often as not they were there as "punishment" for their misbehavior on the settlement. When the outstations at Mangrove were first established, Marguerite had gone to live on one with a couple who had raised her as a child.[14] She had soon returned to the settlement, however, because she found the outstation "boring." In 1981 she told me that she missed the couple because they lived on the station year round, but although she sometimes visted them, she never liked to stay for long.

The absence of school facilities prevented school-age adolescents from staying on the outstations, for parents knew that it was illegal to keep children out of school.[15] Other factors may have kept the older adolescents away. The size of the adolescent peer group was diminished on the outstations by their small populations, and it was likely that a favorite girlfriend or boyfriend would not be present at all. Nor did the outstations have movies, video, or basketball—major amusements of the young. It is likely that other adolescents were also bored by outstation life, and this was one reason for their absence from the stations.

DISCUSSION

In 1981, adolescents like Marguerite, Nora, and Kay belonged to a generation that had spent its entire life on the settlement. They were largely divorced from the life-style of their grandparents and their predecessors—a way of life that had evolved over thousands of years. But the new way of life that the settlement presented to the young had not filled the gap left by the abandonment of the activities, values, and worldview of the nomadic past. Instead, the youth of the settlement seemed as alienated, if not more so, from Western pursuits as they were from their own history. True, they took to such aspects of Western culture as its music, movies, and style of dress, but they were separated by more than geography from the mainstream of white Australia and Western civilization. They seemed to be a puzzle to many of their own elders and to the whites who hoped to instruct them, and were often the concern of both.

Sexual behavior, and the marriage choices it implied, was one domain of adolescent behavior that was a major concern of the older Aboriginal generations at Mangrove. The sexuality of adolescent males may have long been a potential problem for Aboriginal society. In 1981, however, its regulation at Mangrove was probably far more difficult than in the past due to the diminished power of the Law and a weakening of the authority of those who upheld it. As for adolescent girls, the premenarcheal marriage age that once ideally channeled their sexuality in a socially approved direction, was a thing of the past. During the newly prolonged period of maidenhood, female sexual behavior was employed in defiance of parental wishes and marriages were made that ignored many if not all past rules and conventions. In the chapters that follow, these changes in the period of female adolescence and the conflict between generations that they engendered are examined largely in light of the case histories of Marguerite, Nora, and Kay.

■ 3
Marriage Past and Present: The Adult Perspective

This chapter focuses on the historical and cultural factors underlying adult expectations about marriage at Mangrove. After a brief introduction to the politics of Aboriginal marriage, it steps back in time and looks at the marriages of the mothers and grandmothers of Marguerite, Nora, and Kay, for the rules and conditions that generated these unions form a major basis of parental expectations about marriage today.

Marriage in Aboriginal Australia has been described as a male achievement (Merlan 1986, 31; n.d., 14; see also Collier and Rosaldo 1981; Rosaldo 1980). Given the possibility of polygyny and a more or less balanced sex ratio, marriage is not guaranteed for all mature males; the ability of some men to acquire multiple wives (whether through astute political maneuvering, luck, stealth, or force) necessarily entails the continuing bachelorhood of others. Whether men have the right to marry a woman or the right to dispose of a woman in marriage, or whether men arrogate these powers to themselves (Shapiro 1979, 1981, 55; Hiatt 1967, 473–475; Rose 1960, 73–75), male manipulation of females, the giving and taking of wives, is a salient characteristic of Aboriginal social life (see, for example, Hamilton 1974; Hiatt 1965; Hart and Pilling 1960; Rose 1960; Shapiro 1981). Indeed, it has been said that Aboriginal social organization is "centrally and essentially connected with the maintenance, manipulation and transmission" of men's rights in women (Woodburn 1980, in Barnard 1983).

In some Aboriginal groups, Mangrove among them, women are the primary bestowers of such females as their daughters or daughters' daughters. It has been argued, however, that even in this situation, marriage politics are still a male-dominated game insofar as women base their actions on rules that serve male interests more than their own (Bern 1979, 129–130; Cowlishaw 1979, 195–197). Although it is not clear who bestowed the girls in the following case from Gillian Cowlishaw's fieldwork with the Rembarnga, this account illustrates how and why women may act to support male interests with respect to marriage:

> The girls were twelve and fourteen years old respectively, and especially the older one was very reluctant to go to her husband. The girl's labour was useful to the older women but the latter clearly felt anxious about the trouble which might stem from the girls remaining unmarried. The younger girl's mother was anxious that her brother, the girl's MB, would make trouble. The fourteen year old girl had already lived for a short time with her "promise" [betrothed] husband who was about 45, and she had taken advantage of the considerable mobility between communities to move away from him. . . . It was feared that he might attack any one in the camp should the girl not be delivered to him. Again it was the mother who was most anxious that the girl should go to her husband, but also the M"Z" who had brought up the girl from childhood (the mother had eloped), and other 'sisters' were of the same mind. The women's fears were sufficiently strong for the girl to be physically forced to remain with her husband, though she subsequently left him again. (Cowlishaw 1979, 193–194)

Why Aboriginal men are so interested in acquiring wives has been the subject of some discussion in the literature on Aboriginal Australia. A number of writers have emphasized the economic contributions of women (see, for example, Hamilton 1975, 172–173; Hart and Pilling 1960, 34–35, 52; Kaberry 1939, 89–90; Malinowski 1963, 287–288; Meggitt 1965,

155; Radcliffe-Brown 1931, 435). Bronislaw Malinowski, for example, speaking of the "value of a wife to a man," says:

> The woman's work appears as the chief basis of the economy of the Australian household. Her work goes exclusively towards the benefit of the individual family, and this latter economically is entirely dependent upon woman's work. It is her work which, taking to itself the most considerable share in the sexual division of labour, plays the main part in giving to the individual family its economic unity. (Malinowski 1963, 288)

As gatherers of the staple vegetable foods, women once provided the household with its day-to-day subsistence fare. As the "most reliable producers of food," women were the "means of production" and the possession of women made men "strong and independent" (Hamilton 1975, 173). According to C. W. M. Hart and Arnold Pilling:

> The Tiwi themselves had no doubt about the close relationship between plural marriage and good eating. "If I had only one or two wives I would starve," the head of a large household once told the missionary who was preaching against plural marriage, "but with my present ten or twelve wives I can send them out in all directions in the morning and at least two or three of them are likely to bring something back with them at the end of the day, and then we can all eat." (Hart and Pilling 1960, 34)

The labor of young women may be particularly important; by marrying a young girl an old man ensures that he, and his older wife if he has one, will be taken care of (Elkin 1964, 133; Peterson 1974, 22–24).

Some years ago L. R. Hiatt suggested that if we must conjecture about the origins of Aboriginal forms of kinship and marriage, "man's animal nature" might provide a productive starting point (Hiatt 1968, 175). At that time he proposed that in the case of at least one Aboriginal group, "the system of kinship and marriage regulated the distribution of scarce resources in women" (p. 174), thus perhaps minimizing competition between men and the accompanying disruption it can bring to the group. More recently he has suggested that polygyny in Aboriginal Australia can be viewed as a "favoured male reproductive strategy" (Hiatt 1985, 35). That is, as individuals "programmed" to "maximize their own inclusive fitness," Aboriginal men compete with each other, acquiring wives in order to increase the number of their offspring and hence the number of their genes in the next generation (Hiatt 1985, 35; also see Irons 1983).

There is no doubt that many Aboriginal men want children. When, for example, I asked a number of men and women at Mangrove why men wanted more than one wife, the answers boiled down to the following: men wanted children. Men might want several wives in order to have a large family; they might also want a second wife if the first was sterile:

> Some men have a wife and for three or four years she doesn't have a child. "Oh, this girl isn't having my kids, I'll get another wife." So he marries another girl. Might be five or six months and his second wife has a baby. She is going to have a child so she can make a race and a big family. They see when they get old, see their wife having no children. 'I'll have to get another.' (Burbank 1980, 104–105)[1]

Other writers have mentioned the desire for children as a motive for marriage, if not for the accumultation of wives, in Aboriginal Australia (see for example, Berndt 1965b, 81; Kaberry 1939, 90; Meggitt 1962, 96; Warner 1937, 482). A desire for children, however, cannot be equated with a concern with reproductive success. Sociobiologists argue that the motive for a behavior need not be conscious for it to increase the individual's reproductive success and become an integral part of his or her descendant's behavioral repertoire (Daly and Wilson 1983). Possibly polygyny in Aboriginal Australia can be accounted for, at least in part, with reference to a sex-specific human reproductive strategy laid down in our evolutionary past (see Daly and Wilson 1983 for a discussion of this view of human polygyny). This strategy cannot, however, explain why polygyny is "more developed" in Australia than in other hunting and gathering societies (Murdock 1968, 336). Also, given a cultural tradition that often disassociates sexuality from reproduction (Merlan 1986, n.d.) and the widespread opportunities for extramarital sex in Aboriginal Australia (for example, see Hart and Pilling 1960, 79; Goodale 1971, 130–131; Shapiro 1979, 86–88; Malinowski 1963), it is possible that the Aboriginal polygynist of the historical period is no more, and may be even less, successful than an active philanderer.

The productive and reproductive capabilities of Aboriginal women are not all that Aboriginal men may value. Kenneth Maddock, following Claude Lévi-Strauss (1949), sees not only the "use value" of Aboriginal women but also their "exchange value" (Maddock 1972, 64). The conditions of the wandering Aborigine have been depicted by another proponent of alliance theory in the Australian scene:

> In precontact Aboriginal Australia threats to existence would have arisen from a variety of sources—from a particularly harsh environment and unreliable food supply in the face of stone technology, from the relative isolation of the patri-groups and bands (composed of the males of a patri-group, their wives and unmarried children) often spread over vast areas, and from occasionally vengeful and belligerent outsiders whose customs possibly differed qualitatively from one's own and who sometimes found themselves with a deficit of suitably related marriageable women. (Turner 1980, xi)

The solution to such problems of existence is the exchange of women between what now become exogamous but allied groups. Insofar as the marriage destinies of women can be directed, they "widen and pattern sociality"; their unions become symbols of the alliances that allow the exogamous groups the environmental flexibility they need to survive (Maddock 1972, 35, 46, 64; see also Sackett 1976, 146–147). Hiatt (1965, 1967, 1968) and Shapiro (1979, 89–99; 1981) have demonstrated at length the shortcomings of alliance theory in the contexts of specific Aboriginal marriage arrangements. Their arguments do not lead to the conclusion that alliances are never formed in Aboriginal society (see, for example, Keen 1982, 632; also see Needham 1986 and Keen 1986, 226–227 on the ambiguity of the word *alliance*), or that the idea of exchange is not important to Aboriginal people (see the discussion later in this chapter), but rather that the theory itself cannot greatly advance our understanding of Aboriginal culture or behavior because its inherent assumptions about Aboriginal social organization are not supported by the evidence of Aboriginal ethnography. (For a rebuttal of Hiatt 1967, see Maddock 1969; for a rebuttal of Maddock, see Shapiro 1981, 101–102; also see Keen 1986, 223–228.)

Which brings me to the topic of the games people play, specifically to the games of Aboriginal men. Warren Shapiro has recently reminded us of Kroeber's suggestion that the elaboration of Aboriginal kinship might just be play (Kroeber 1952, 218, in Shapiro 1979, 81). Along similar lines, Aboriginal marriage politics might be seen as a game and the accumulation of women as a sign of a player's success; men might value women for the status and prestige that accrues for simply doing well in a game where women are the stakes. Hart and Pilling, for example, see Aboriginal women as the "main 'trumps' in the endless bridge game" whose prize is power and influence (1960, 52). Frederick Rose has interpreted the male attitude toward polygyny along similar lines. From Rose's Marxist perspective, polygyny is a female invention, arising from their need for co-wives to help with the burdens of childcare (Rose 1960, 241; 1968, 206; see also Irons 1983). This adaptive arrangement is the "social being" that determines male consciousness, hence the jealous male's "desire . . . to monopolize the women" (Rose 1960, 174). In short, Aboriginal men may attempt to accumulate wives simply because it is the name of the game in their society.

In all likelihood the reasons that Aboriginal men attempt to accumulate and control women are many—distal and proximate, both conscious and unconscious to the individuals that they motivate. Whatever these reasons might be, one thing is clear: this male-dominated activity requires the compliance of Aboriginal women (Merlan 1986, 35–36). As Maddock has put it, "Were women free to marry as they wished . . . they would be less useful as objects of exchange" (Maddock 1972, 46).

Summarizing the ethnography of gender in Aboriginal society, Francesca Merlan has observed that when it comes to marriage, older women are less likely than younger ones to acquiesce to arrangements made on their behalf (Merlan 1986, 35; see also White 1974, 21; Goodale 1971, 228; Bell 1980; Hamilton 1974). As will be seen later in the chapter, at least some of the Aboriginal women of Mangrove would agree with this assertion. Thus marriages based on bestowing young, and probably more compliant, girls are particularly important, for in these men can acquire power, if not wives, both through "claims upon the women themselves, and the accompanying reciprocal claims of affines upon each other" (Merlan 1986, 32). Thus at Mangrove, where, as we see in the next two chapters, girls are far from acquiescent when it comes to their bestowal, it should not be surprising that marriage has become a focal point of conflict between the generations.

MARRIAGE AT MANGROVE: THE IDEALS OF PAST AND PRESENT

There are six characteristics of the ideal marriage system of the past as it was explained to me by some of Mangrove's older residents. These characteristics were, at one time, widespread throughout the continent (see for example, Maddock 1972; Shapiro 1979, 1981). These form the background of expectations in contemporary marriage negotiations and must be mentioned, if just briefly. They are

1. All women are married.
2. Females join their husbands before menarche.
3. The arrangement of a marriage is not the sole concern of potential partners. A female's marriage is ideally arranged by her matrikin.
4. The selection of partners is governed by rules of partner selection that define which partners are "straight" and "not straight" (see below).
5. Females are exchanged in marriage.
6. Marriages may be polygynous.

In the past, or so say older people at Mangrove today, two women and their mothers and mothers' brothers might decide that they would make their respective children, a "little boy" and a "little girl," *gajali,* that is, mother-in-law and son-in-law together.[2] In a brief ritual, one or another of these people would rub white clay into the children's hair. The clay ensured that the "promise" the relationship entailed would not be forgotten. When the little girl grew, married, and had children, she would give all of her daughters to this son-in-law as his wives. Ideally, this son-in-law was an eldest son and if, or when, he died, these women were to go to his surviving brothers. This act also entailed reciprocity. If the son-in-law had a sister, she was to give all her daughters as wives to her brother's mother-in-law's brother (see also Heath 1980, 333; Shapiro 1970, 62–63, 1981; Goodale 1971, 50–52).

A group of older women told me about this brief ritual. They said it was no longer performed but added, "We still follow *gajali* way," referring to the form of marriage associated with the contract and the ritual. A woman who decided that her daughter was to be a mother-in-law could not simply choose a son-in-law for her at random. She had to ensure that her granddaughters would be married correctly, to a man their mother called *gajali* ("MMBS") because she called his father *gagu* ("MMB"). This is what is meant by "marriage *gajali* way."

The father of a woman's son-in-law should come from the same country as her mother's mother, but should not share a parent with her. A man could have as many mothers-in-law to give him wives as he had *gajali* of this kind.

Only one person, an older woman in her late fifties, told me that she had seen children made *gajali.* This was when she was a "little girl," perhaps forty-five or fifty years ago. Younger people said that they had only heard of the ritual from their mothers and grandmothers. The extent to which the contract it represents was employed as a means of establishing marriages is impossible to know. However, the model of marriage it implies still informed the thought and behavior of the people of Mangrove in 1981.

Marriage histories of the women at Mangrove indicate that in a more recent period, around the time that Sandy Creek Mission was established, girls were bestowed when they were infants or little girls. Straight marriage, however, continued to be marriage *gajali* way. To ensure a correct marriage a woman would bestow her daughter on her *gajali.* But as was the case when mothers-in-law were bestowed, she would not bestow her on an actual MMBS. A woman would not even call the children of her actual MMB *gajali*; instead she would call them *gagu* as she would their father. On the other hand, a woman should give her daughters to a man whose father was "really" her "MMB," that is, to a man from the same country as her actual mother's mother.[3]

If a classificatory "MMBS" were not available, a woman might bestow her daughter on one of her classificatory "brother's sons." In this case neither partner should share a country with their parents-in-law. Today this form is called "marriage auntie way," "auntie" being the Kriol term for "father's sister," the category of woman who gives a man his wife.

According to the majority of my informants, a girl is most properly bestowed by her mother and mother's brothers. As Nora's mother once put it, it is this pair that are "really responsible" (see also Heath 1980, 337). My data on the role of fathers are more equivocal. Some women said that a man has the right to join with his wife and her brother in the bestowal of his daughters.[4] Others said that fathers should just "listen" and stand behind the decisions made by their wives and brothers-in-law. (For discussions of varying conceptualizations of marriage in Aboriginal society, see Hamilton 1974; Shapiro 1977; Hiatt 1967).

When asked about bestowal rights, Marguerite's mother, Lily, emphasized a mother's role: "Mother really is boss. She had the pain [of childbirth] and she did the work [of child rearing]." Other women may share Lily's perception of mothers as central figures in the matter of bestowals. For example, out of forty-three marriage histories collected from women informants in 1977–1978, mothers were said to have taken some action with respect to the marriages of their daughters in thirty instances, whereas a mother's brother was mentioned in only one case (Burbank 1980, 77–80). Why women attribute formal control to mothers' brothers but emphasize the effective control of mothers is unclear. What is important here, however, particularly in light of the material presented in chapter 4, is the indication that women assign priority to themselves in the marriage arrangements of their daughters (cf. Hamilton 1974).

A girl's bestowers should not take unilateral action whoever they might be. They are expected to consult with others before making or acting upon a decision. Generally these others were described as a girl's "family," like her father's sisters, mother's mother, mother's mother's brother, mother's father, and mother's father's sister. The people who dreamt (see below) a girl should also be consulted. Later in this work when I use the word *parent,* as I do merely for convenience, I am referring to those senior kin who have authority in a girl's marriage.

The exchange of women is a primary consideration in marriage arrangements (see also Turner 1974, 48). Exchange was spoken of in two ways, as "*laga* for *laga,*" that is, "sister for sister" or as "*ngura* to *ngura,*" that is, exchange of the sort that followed the bestowal of a mother-in-law (see also Heath 1980, 343).[5] The following conversation about a marriage that would not take place because of a failure to "square back" mentions both these forms and demonstrates the salience of this principle:

■ *Did you hear that Herman was making trouble? He ran off with Marylou. . . .*

Herman and Marylou are straight. Why don't they give her to him?

Because Jules has her elder sister, and the Law is that the man who marries the eldest sister gets all the sisters. . . . [But] Jules didn't square back for his wife, so Marylou's uncles are blocking him from getting Marylou. He could give one of his sisters' children. . . . He is a millionaire Jules; he has four sisters and two of them have daughters.

Well if Marylou's uncles don't want Jules because he didn't square back, why don't they let her marry Herman?

Because Herman doesn't have any sisters to square back. . . . If Herman had sisters they would let him and Marylou marry because Jules doesn't square back.

Brothers, however, do not as a rule dispose of their sisters in marriage or have the right to do so. If Herman had sisters, it would be up to their bestowers to decide if they should be given in exchange for Marylou.

At times, exchange may even be more important than rules of partner selection: "If a man gets a woman who is not quite straight for him and that woman has a brother, the first man will give that brother his sister to marry. They will be square and there will be no trouble. As long as they square back, then it will be all right. This is what they mean when they say, 'Fire made it straight.'"

THE IDEAL MARRIAGE AGE

To illustrate the ideal marriage age for females in pre-mission times, older Aboriginal women pointed to girls between the ages of nine and fourteen. None of these girls had yet reached the stage of breast development associated by Aboriginal women with the approach of menarche.

As I have said before, there is, unfortunately, no ethnographic data from this period, and thus it is difficult to confirm, or cast doubt on, these statements about a premenarcheal age of marriage. However, reports on Aboriginal groups living in nearby areas before European presence greatly disturbed Aboriginal social forms provide some corroboration. Warner, for example, worked in the Milingimbi area of Northeast Arnhem Land, about 150 miles away from Mangrove, only three years after the area's first white outpost, a Methodist mission, was established in 1923. He reports: "The proper time for a girl to marry is when her breasts first start developing" and adds, "A young girl often starts living in her husband's household before menstruation" (Warner 1937, 118, 65). Evidence also comes from Rose who worked on Groote Eylandt in 1941. He states that girls married at about the age of nine, years before menarche, which he estimates occurred between the ages of thirteen and fourteen (Rose 1960, 65, 67). An Anglican mission had been established on the island twenty years before Rose's study, but it served only an immigrant "half-caste" population until 1933. Aboriginal families began to take up residence on the mission in 1937, but it was not until 1949 that mission records stated that Aboriginal people were no longer living in the bush (Rose 1960, 13–14; Turner 1974, 13). Though missionaries had worked with the Tiwi for years before her study, Goodale reports that Tiwi girls were delivered to their husbands before puberty (Goodale 1971, 43–45). Missionaries present in the early days of Sandy Creek Mission at Mangrove said that they had seen girls married between the ages of eight and fourteen. As mentioned in chapter 1, menarche at Mangrove today likely occurs between the ages of thirteen and fourteen and may have occurred at a somewhat later age when the Aborigines of the area were still nomads.[6]

Aboriginal women explained that early marriage ensured that a girl would settle with her intended husband. As one woman put it, "The little girl didn't have sense to think about it and say no."[7] At a later age she might decide on another man or against marriage itself, breaking the contract and creating complications in the marriages of others.

ROSALIND'S MARRIAGE

Such threats to the system, threats that are associated with a girl's maturing sexuality and resolve, may be seen in the case of Rosalind's marriage. Rosalind had not been promised when she was a little girl. Her mother ran away from Rosalind's father when Rosalind was about nine years of age, leaving the child with her father. He, in turn, placed her in the care of one of his classificatory brothers and wife, who were then living on a mission about one hundred miles from Mangrove. This couple, Rosalind's classificatory "mother" and "father," arranged her marriage when she was about fourteen years of age. According to Rosalind, their decision to do so was precipitated by her developing relationship with a young man they did not approve of as a marriage partner for their ward. They did not, she explained, like his family. This probably means that he was not straight, that is, he was an inappropriate partner according to the rules of partner selection. Instead, Rosalind's "father" arranged for Rosalind to marry his "close" "mother's brother," Greenleaf, who was then about nineteen years of age. Rosalind was in the mission school at the time. "You are not going to have school now. You are going to get married now," her guardians informed her. Rosalind, however, replied, "No, I'm not going to marry that man!" She didn't know him, she'd never even seen him, and besides, she liked her "friend." He had been "looking after" her from the time she was "little," buying her presents from the shop, and, at the time that her "mother" and "father" intervened, she "was nearly married" to him. Her guardians continued to press the suit of Greenleaf, and Rosalind continued to resist. However, her boyfriend went to an Aboriginal settlement about two hundred miles away, and her guardians said, "Before he comes back he's going to see you married." And shortly before he did return, Rosalind decided that she would have to say yes to their proposal.

It was Rosalind's guardians' right to arrange this marriage since Rosalind had no promise and they had raised her, but Rosalind's mother's close classificatory brother, the son of her mother's sister, chose this time to say that he wanted a wife and would "block" the marriage of Rosalind and Greenleaf if he did not get one. He was given one of Greenleaf's sister's daughters as a wife, so he and Rosalind's mother did not prohibit Rosalind's marriage as they might have.

The mission's chaplain was asked to marry the couple and did so in September of 1947. When Rosalind's boyfriend finally returned he was "upset" with her family, but by then Rosalind was living on another mission with her husband and his family.

Rosalind, however, kept "remembering" her boyfriend and her family. Eventually she "forgot" but not until her first child was born in 1950. She describes those early days of marriage and her relations with her husband:

> when [Greenleaf] used to make his bed, I never went to him when it was still early. I let him sleep. Then when I saw he was fast asleep I used to crawl over. Auntie used to tell me, "Go sleep now, it's the middle of the night." "No, I'm gonna sit here by the fire. I'm cold." When I did go and sleep beside him and felt him touching my body, I wrapped myself up in my blanket [and rolled away from him]. And Auntie would say, "Oh, look at that girl."

THE MARRIAGE OF MARGUERITE'S MATERNAL GRANDMOTHER

In the ideal past, a girl would not feel about her husband as Rosalind felt about Greenleaf in the early days of her marriage.

A man who acquired a mother-in-law, whether directly through her bestowal or indirectly through the bestowal of a wife, also acquired an obligation to provide her with food, and in recent times, with such things as tobacco, clothing, and money.[8] The fulfillment of these obligations would bring him to his mother-in-law's camp, providing opportunities for a girl to become acquainted with her husband before she actually joined him as a wife. The girl's mother might encourage the relationship, sending her daughter to her future husband to receive his contributions or to play around his camp. Sometimes a sleeping girl would be carried over to her husband to sleep by his fire until morning, returning to her family the next day. The man might also carry his young wife on his shoulder when the group moved. Marguerite's maternal grandmother describes how she felt about her husband before she joined his household: "I wasn't frightened of my husband before we were married. I fed him, gave him a hand, went and sat down there with him. My mother cooked food for him, I took the food. I told Lily to go take her husband food and drink."[9]

Marguerite's grandmother was promised to her husband by her mother's second husband when she was a "little girl." She joined him as a wife, by her own report, when she was about the size of a contemporary fifteen-year-old, a girl who may or may not have begun to menstruate. At the time of the marriage, this man had two other wives, two sisters. The eldest of these women had been married previously, twice in fact, to two classificatory brothers. She had borne them four children, one of whom was Rosalind's mother. The three women did not live together for long, however. Marguerite's grandfather informed his two older wives that he had "another one" and so they could "stay single." The eldest of the two did just that. "All right, you can take my granddaughter now to be your wife, and I'm going to stay single," reported Rosalind of her grandmother's words at the time.[10] She slept apart from her husband and his new wife, Marguerite's grandmother, but continued to receive meat, fish, and other things from him. The younger sister left, however, and eventually remarried.

For a time Marguerite's grandfather worked on the various mission boats that delivered supplies, mail, and personnel from one area mission to another. Possibly his separation from two women who together had borne him four living children was a response to increasing pressure for monogamous unions. This pressure, at least in its institutionalized forms, was largely a product of mission initiative. But perhaps Marguerite's grandmother also encouraged her husband in this direction. Again Rosalind speaks: "Some women are happy like that, they can stay one fire [together in the same camp], but that young girl may be jealous, 'I don't want this old woman to stay with us, send her away.'"[11]

Whether the Aboriginal women in this part of Australia were content with their polygynous unions or chafed in this form of marriage is just one of the many questions whose answers are lost to history. Whether mission doctrine was bolstered by a preexisting antipathy or whether mission doctrine created that antipathy is likewise a question that cannot really be answered. As I indicated in chapter 2, mission regulation was gradually decreased and government policies in the 1970s and 1980s gave more recognition to the legitimacy of at least some Aboriginal forms of social organization. By 1981 polygyny was no longer discouraged by the white authorities, but it is clear that many, if not all of the women of Mangrove favored monogamy. Here Lily speaks about a return to the former arrangement: "These men are talking about having more wives. How do they think they are going to feed all those children." And here Marguerite speaks: "I don't like [polygyny]. I don't like to share a man with anybody."

David Turner has suggested that the sort of argument against polygyny presented here by Lily was originated by missionaries, at least on Groote Eylandt (1974, 51). His suggestion is supported by an entry in the Sandy Creek superintendent's journal on May 2, 1970, "I said govt only pays pension for 1 wife and if a lot of wives hard for a man to look after them."

DEVIATIONS FROM THE IDEAL IN CONTEMPORARY UNIONS

In 1981 the unions of Mangrove's population deviated in at least two ways from the ideal model of marriage. On the whole, contemporary marriages are not polygynous. They also often consist of partners who have not been chosen for each other, but rather who have chosen each other.

In March of 1981 twenty-three adult women at Mangrove were reported to have lived "one fire" in a polygynous marriage at some point in their marital histories.[12] Twenty-two of these women were born before 1936 and in 1952, the year that Sandy Creek Mission was established, were at least sixteen, well past the ideal age of marriage. The twenty-two women born before 1936, and thus over the age of forty-six in 1981, represent 65 percent of this age-sex group living at Mangrove in March of 1981. In the sixteen polygynous marriages that I recorded for these twenty-three women, they shared a husband with a minimum of one co-wife and a maximum of six co-wives, at least twenty-five of whom were no longer living by 1981.

In contrast, none of the eighty marriages in effect in 1981 were polygynous in the sense implied by the term "one fire," that is, where all the women lived together with their husband in one camp.[13] Only one man was said to have more than one wife, and only one of them lived at Mangrove.

Over a third of the eighty marriages in effect at Mangrove in 1981, or twenty-eight, consisted of couples who had chosen their own partners. This number is likely a conservative estimate for marriage histories were obtained for only forty-eight of the eighty unions.[14] Data indicate that at least another seven cases might be included, but as they are not conclusive I present the lower figure. Incomplete though it may be, this picture represents a distinct deviation from the ideal of arranged marriage; how much of a deviation from actual behavior in earlier times is an open question, however.

The age distribution of the women in these unions of choice suggests, however, that they may indeed be the new phenomenon they are perceived to be by older Aborigines who decry the laxity of current social forms. All but two of the women in marriages of choice were between the ages of fifteen and thirty-nine. That is, all but two were born after 1941 and were no older than ten in 1952. The majority were far from nubile when the mission was first established. One of the two older women was in her second marriage which was contracted during the mission period. The second older woman had, like Rosalind's mother, run away from her first husband with her present husband at least thirty years ago. This distribution of the ages of women in marriages of choice is almost a mirror image of that of women who were once in polygynous marriages, which strongly suggests that this characteristic of present-day marriage, like monogamy, is a recent development associated more with current than past conditions of social life.

THE MISSION AND MARRIAGE

The most obvious influence on current conditions is, of course, all that is implied by the word *pre-mission*. Prior to 1952 there was no European outpost of any sort in the area. After 1952, there was the Sandy Creek Mission at Mangrove. Aboriginal people largely attributed changes in their form of marriage to the mission situation, if not specifically to the policies and rules of the missionaries themselves.

That the missionaries were concerned with aspects of the indigenous marriage system and attempted to eradicate such practices as infant betrothal, polygyny, and premenarcheal marriage age are indicated by various records and documents from the mission period. For example, one of the recommendations made by a missionary delegation to a nearby mission in 1940 reads: "Re Child Marriages, Tribal: When the girls on the station are married—very often to men much older than themselves—much of the work of the missionary is lost. In view of our experience we would urge that the missionaries explore the possibility of 'purchasing' if necessary, the right of consent to marry" (quoted in Cole 1977, 193).

In suggesting that mission personnel purchase marriage rights to women, this delegation was likely following the example of Father Gsell, a Catholic missionary who began work with the Tiwi of Bathurst Island (off the coast from Darwin) in 1911. Father Gsell's campaign against polygyny and arranged marriage led to his reputation as "the Bishop with 150 Wives." He "bought" young Tiwi girls from their fathers or husbands with axes, cloth, tobacco, flour, and other material objects, thus freeing them to choose their own husbands when they came of age by mission standards (Hart and Pilling 1960, 101–102).

The idea of barter or purchase was also used on another mission in the area, established by the same missionaries who had set up Mangrove. Among their attempts to redistribute wives, they "bought" women from older men with several wives, then gave them to younger men with none. At least eight men gave up nine women who were then married to nine other men, though one woman was later reclaimed by her original husband (Turner 1974, 51). Lily, who was between the ages of seven and ten at the time, tells the tale of this redistribution: "The missionary took those wives from those old men with three or four and gave them to other men. Some of the men got angry. One tried to cut him with a tommy hawk. [My mother] helped him give those women. Some stayed, some didn't. He gave [my auntie]. He gave the men tobacco, flour, tommy hawks."

No such distribution was attempted at Mangrove, but in the opinion of a chaplain present in 1956, the Sandy Creek people were impressed by the events on the neighboring mission where wives had been redistributed. The first mission official at Sandy Creek Mission told his flock that polygyny was not consistent with a Christian way of life. On the other mission the missionaries said they would leave if the men did not give up some of their wives (Burbank 1980, 82). Whether or not a similar argument was used at Mangrove is unknown. However, as there has always been considerable visiting back and forth between the people of the various area missions, the people of Mangrove likely heard of the missionaries' resolve to leave if at least some women were not redistributed.

There are no records of early mission action with respect to Aboriginal marriage arrangements at Mangrove, but later documents indicate the manner and extent to which the missionaries attempted to change the indigenous system. For example, here are some excerpts from a paper titled "Materials for Teaching on Native Marriage" attached to the mission's monthly report for February 1959:

Who instituted marriage? Gen 2:18–24
What did our Lord say about this? Mat 19:4–6
How many wives? Gen 2:18 again: Adam and Eve
Every man should be able to have a wife and every woman a husband.

St. Paul and Ephesians 5:24: One Xt . . .
What of polygamous households?
    a. a wife may be baptized; the husband may not if he
       has more than one wife (except on deathbed?)
    b. the husband may agree to release all but one wife,
       but another husband should be found for her, ac-
       cording to right kinship classification.

Is it right to promise a girl to a man?
    Yes, but she must agree, therefore not infant betrothal.
    Gen 24:58 (or possibly translate whole story)

Apparently a purchaselike strategy was also tried at Mangrove. The March 1962 monthly report includes this paragraph:

> Meetings were held to discuss with the people the recent
> suggestion by the Chaplains with regard to reimbursement
> to men of money [5.0.0] in return for the giving up of rights
> to a Promise. A time limit was set and 6 men signed agree-
> ments to do this. It is expected that the husband of the girl
> will pay to the Mission the sum of £ 5.0.0 when his mar-
> riage is arranged by the people.

A chaplain's report for July 1968 suggests that the campaign against polygyny and arranged marriage continued into
the 1960s:

> The Promise system was discussed and a special meeting
> held in the . . . Village to talk about several problems con-
> cerning this. The conference also re-affirmed that "One
> man one wife" was a good principle to continue on our
> mission.
>
>   Several Christian young people may be married soon
> if all parties are happy. Such matters are a real problem
> because so many people want to have a say and such mar-
> riages may be held up indefinitely because someone
> objects for some reason. This was one reason why the Cer-
> emonies Conference suggested a dropping of the promise
> system and allowing young people to make their own
> choice of partners. However such choices would need to be
> "straight" from the kinship point of view to please most I
> would think.

That mission policy on Aboriginal marriage did not go entirely unchallenged by Aboriginal people is suggested by two entries in the mission superintendent's daily journal, one as late as 1970, the other in 1961:

> May 2, 1970: [At a meeting for councillors about the marriage of a young woman, an Aboriginal man] asked me about this mission rule only 1 wife. I said [the first mission official] did talk to the people . . . and I thought [M] could tell him about this and what was said and agreed. I said govt only pays pension for 1 wife and if a lot of wives hard for a man to look after them. After meeting I asked [man who wanted to marry the young woman] if the Conference had agreed 1 man 1 wife. He said yes. I said do you agree with this. He said yes. . . .

> August 11, 1961: Some men requested meeting with Welfare officers to discuss "this mission law" namely
>   1. no exceeding of 2 lb per week ration of sugar
>   2. limit of 2 × 3 lbs of flour per week per adult
>   3. 1 man 1 wife
> Meeting held. Mr. [Chaplain] present—main objectors [list of four men].

What appears to be the welfare officer's reply to the third query is recorded in an entry on November 4, 1961:

> Promise Mission rule explained but Govt has no such rule. Those who want another wife can leave mission and live on Govt Settlement or Darwin.

A MISSION MARRIAGE: THE CASE OF LILY

Mission efforts to change Aboriginal marriage practices continued through the 1970s. Their effects, however, were apparent much earlier. The marriage of Lily in January of 1953 and that of her younger sister in 1956 are two cases in point. Lily's mother bestowed Lily upon a correct marriage partner when she was an infant. Before she was given to her betrothed, however, he married her elder half sister. Lily's mother then promised Lily to Goodman. She also promised one of Lily's younger sisters to another man. But the younger sister never joined her promise as a wife and married Goodman's younger brother instead. Lily said that her sister did not marry her original betrothed because "the missionaries said men can only have one wife." Of the changes in her own marital history and of her first betrothed Lily said, "He was really a nice man, but I was too young to go to him then and he got [my half sister]."

Both Lily and her sister married at the age of sixteen, the legal age of marriage with parental consent under white Australian law and at least several years later than the Aboriginal ideal. A former missionary, Mangrove's superintendent from 1959 to 1976, spoke to me about marriage age and related matters. The notes I took of our conversation are reproduced here:

■ *One area that I would like to know more about is marriage age. My impression is that it has changed and I wonder if you could tell me anything about this and its source?*

We tried to influence this. When we heard that a girl was going to be married and we thought she was too young we would talk to her parents, perhaps her mother if she spoke English and her father didn't. We were concerned about the health of the girl and so we would ask them to wait until the girl was a little older.

How old?

Sixteen.

Was this arbitrary or because it was the legal age of marriage in Australia?

I think because it was the legal age.

How old were the girls that parents were trying to marry?

Oh, about thirteen or fourteen. Often the parents didn't know how old the girls were. But because the children were in our charge and we had to keep records on how old they were . . . we did. We only had to talk to a few parents, most seemed to catch on and most waited until the girls were sixteen. Although one time we spoke to a girl's mother and thought everything was all set and then we were horrified to discover that the girl had been allowed to spend the night

> *alone in a house. That was regarded as a marriage cere-*
> *mony so there was nothing we could do, they were married.*
> *In some instances we offered girls protection when they*
> *didn't want to marry a very old man, or when they were*
> *afraid the man to whom they had been promised would*
> *take them by force or give them a hiding.*
>
> *What do you mean by protection?*
>
> *Sanctuary. They would come down to the European part of*
> *the village to escape the man for that night. We sympa-*
> *thized with girls who didn't want to join very old men, but*
> *we didn't feel they had a right to just say, "I want that*
> *young man." But when they came to us, we couldn't turn*
> *them away.*

Note that if a nubile girl refused to join her betrothed, it was regarded as appropriate for him to abduct her, especially if her
mother sent word to her son-in-law to come "pull out" his wife
(Burbank 1980, 118–119). The missionaries, however, did not
approve of such strategies for marrying off shy or recalcitrant
girls. A further example is provided by an entry in the Mangrove
superintendent's journal for February 12, 1964: "Letter sent to
policeman as [M] said she was not willing to humbug [have in-
tercourse] and [D, her promise] forced her. Told [D] wait until
police come." Turner reports similar responses to abduction on
the part of the Groote Eylandt missionaries (1974, 63–64).

The date of the first marriage for fifty of Mangrove's currently married women is known. For these women, all married at one of the three area settlements, the median marriage
age is sixteen, the mean seventeen, and the range thirteen to
twenty-four.

THE MISSION AND MARRIAGES OF CHOICE

Among the entries in the superintendent's journals is a series
that tells the story of a marriage of choice. This story suggests
the kinds of experiences that form part of the cultural context in
which Mangrove's adolescent girls, and their parents, contem-
plate marriage today. The story concerns four people, Bill, a

man then about thirty-two years of age, Jake, a man of unknown age, Paul, a "young boy" of twenty when he makes his
appearance in this story, and Merilee, a girl between the ages of
fourteen and fifteen when the series of recorded events began
in 1960. Merilee was betrothed to Bill. Apparently, the series of
events recorded by the superintendent began when Bill attempted to take his young promised wife:

23-2-60
Argument in camp about [Merilee] and [Bill] marriage. [S]
says [A] could marry this girl but he did not say anything
when the matter was first agreed to by Mr. [Chaplain], Mr.
[Superintendent], [D], [L]. . . .

31-12-60
Argument about [Merilee] and [Jake].

1-1-61
[Merilee] says she wants to marry [Bill].

13-1-61
Fight in afternoon, [Jake] and [Bill] re [Merilee]. In morning Mr. [Chaplain] and I spoke to [Bill] and [D] and agreed
to marriage of [Bill] and [Merilee]. When we saw [Merilee]
at hospital she said no. Had been talk of her and [Jake].
[Bill] hit [Jake]. Camp in uproar. . . .

27-8-61
Meeting re [Merilee]. Was with [Bill] last night but did not
humbug. Said she didn't want to marry him so meeting told
of this decision.

18-9-61
[Bill] took [Merilee] at night. She was taken to mission
house for protection.

25-9-61
Talk to [Bill]. Told to leave [Sandy Creek] and go to [an-
other mission]. Went with [two clan brothers].

12-5-62
Meeting re [Jake] and [Merilee] . . . [Merilee] says she does
not want [Jake].

Entries about Merilee end here but resume six years later with
the following:

19-5-68
[Paul] and [Merilee] ran away on Friday night.

22-5-68
Interview with [Paul] and asked him what he did last Friday and Saturday.

2-12-68
[Paul] and [Merilee] off again to bush.

Around this time the chaplain's report also made note of the affair:

Recently we have been saddened by the loss of three Sunday School teachers. . . . [Merilee] also has had marriage problems but her choice is not "straight" in the view of the relations and they too have run off on a number of occasions. She and [Paul] are also out of fellowship (January 1969).

Returning to the superintendent's journal:

30-4-69
[Paul] and [Merilee] repeatedly running off together. Village had meeting last night.

6-5-69
Visit by [Paul] to ask for job back. Had long talk to warn how he has upset people. He said he had come back and would leave [Merilee] now. He said only his mother objecting. I believe she's frightened of [Bill]. I asked how he thought I could help him. He said he did not know. I said see me again if I can help you.

31-5-69
[Paul]/[Merilee] away together.

16-7-69
During day [Paul's] swag removed from beach. [Paul] upset when he returned. Saw him in Village with spears. Spoke to him and asked him to come and talk quietly to me. He said yes and we talked near the church. I asked if he would like me to talk to the Counsellors. He said you can try. He left and walked back quietly to the Village. Truly the Lord is the one who listens and gives peace. Praise him. I saw [Paul's half brother and father's brother] and asked them to

find out what the trouble was. They said they were happy about [Merilee] and [Paul] and I said let me know after you talked in the Village. That night they came to my house with uncles and in the back ground a bride and bridegroom. I was told it was all sorted out. Old people had been afraid as "someone said [a group of people] going to spear you." So they separated the couple and their swags. Told [Paul] and [Merilee] to come back and see me and tell me they were married so I could record it.

In the case of Paul and Merilee the missionaries supported a union they knew to be incorrect by Aboriginal standards. There are indications, however, that they gave some recognition to the rules governing marriage partner selection and even acted in terms of this recognition. For example, recall the suggestion in the "Materials for Teaching on Native Marriage" that redistributed women should marry someone of the right "kinship classification."

Respect for Aboriginal marriage rules was not always characteristic of mission action in the area, however. Turner, for example, makes the following observation of the Aborigines on Groote Eylandt: "It appears that for a certain period of time the Aborigines became convinced, partly through the insistence of Whites and partly through their own insight, that their assumptions about 'closeness' (which underlay their definition of prohibited marriages) were to some extent 'incorrect.' . . . The attitude of the missionaries toward the Aboriginal notion of 'closeness' here is implied in the following quotation from the mission records (1954): 'Meeting of the men held in evening re dispute amongst some about the advisability of Naingabara marrying Polly. It was thought that his father and her mother were brother and sister. This was later disproved and now all are satisfied'" (Turner 1974, 62–63).

Some of the most notorious misalliances from the Aboriginal perspective were made by Aborigines closely associated with the missionaries. At Mangrove, for example, banns were published in 1968 for Lyle and Margot, a young couple active in church affairs. The superintendent noted of the banns that "some objected"; indeed Lyle and Margot did not succeed in marrying until 1970, and only then by running away, in spite of apparent church support. This couple is regarded as incorrect because Lyle married his "close" "mother's brother's daughter." The extent to which this marriage is perceived as "really wrong" is indicated by the fact that Lyle's relationship to Margot was hurled at him as an imprecation in a fight that took place in 1978, eight years after the marriage.

WRONG WAY MARRIAGE

Mission efforts alone, however, do not explain all of the changes in marriage that have occured at Mangrove. Some of the impetus for change must be attributed to the Aborigines themselves. The mission provided such settings as school and church for the romances of couples like Merilee and Paul and Lyle and Margot, and enough weight in the balance that such romances could become marriages. But the mission did not push Merilee and Paul or Lyle and Margot into their affairs in the first place. The mission provided a situation that could be capitalized on by young women who did not want to marry the men they were assigned to and by young men who might otherwise have to wait for years before marrying anyone. And people did capitalize on the situation if the twenty-eight marriages of choice are any indication.

The question is Did people in pre-mission times likewise attempt to manipulate circumstances to achieve similar ends? (For discussions of this question in other Aboriginal communities see Hiatt 1968; Kaberry 1939; Meggitt 1965; Piddington 1970; Sackett 1975–1976.) A high proportion of incorrect marriages in the pre-mission population would indicate that they did. Again, however, actual behavior in pre-mission times is difficult to ascertain. The Aborigines of my acquaintance tended to shun conversation of "wrong" marriages both past and present, and the genealogical depth necessary to trace the relationships of a significant number of couples married in pre-mission times was beyond the memory of my informants. However, in the cases of fifty-five women, both living and dead, born no later than 1937 and probably married before mission influence had much impact on marriage, I was able to ascertain whether one of the spouses shared a country with his or her parents-in-law. Recall that a country would not be shared in a "straight" marriage. An analysis of these marriages showed that in only two cases, or 4 percent, did one partner share the country of his or her mother-in-law (see also Shapiro 1970). There were no cases of intramoiety marriage.

In sixty-nine of the eighty marriages in effect at Mangrove in 1981, I was also able to ascertain if either spouse shared a country with a parent-in-law. Four spouses did so, or about 6 percent of the cases. Taken alone this number does not seem to show a significant increase in incorrect unions. However, there were two intramoiety marriages among the eighty marriages in effect in 1981. There were also at least fourteen other marriages labeled by one person or another as "not straight." In five of these cases the partners were linked genealogically to a degree regarded by Aborigines as "too close" for affinal partners. For example, in one of these unions a man was married to his actual MMBDD. In eight cases, however, it is unclear why these unions should be labeled as they were.

I cannot say with certainty that these twenty marriages exhaust the universe of such unions in effect in 1981. As indicated, information about incorrect unions was hard to come by; it was not a subject to be broached directly. Most of the information acquired on current incorrect unions was volunteered (see also Sackett 1975–1976, 45).

THE LEGITIMACY OF CHOICE

At least fifteen of the twenty "not straight" marriages were marriages of choice, and at least six of the eight cases where it is unclear why the union is labeled "not straight" were marriages of choice. These six cases consist of couples who either ran off together and married in spite of parental opposition, married after leaving a husband or wife (supposedly a new and clearly a disapproved form of behavior), or broke other rules of custom and etiquette in forming a union. (In the remaining two cases the man did not marry his original betrothed, but another woman instead, which suggests that these were also marriages of choice. But since the case material is inconclusive the cases are not included.) The circumstances in which these six marriages were made and the designation "not straight" that is attached to them suggest that the label is applied not only to unions that do not conform to rules designating correct partners, but also to marriages that do not conform to rules for arranging a union.

There are a number of indications that in 1981 the absence or presence of parental approval or consent to a son's or daughter's marriage was one of the criteria for judging the legitimacy of a union. This may be stated in a revised version of the third characteristic of marriage presented at the beginning of this chapter:

> The arrangement of marriage is not the sole concern of potential marriage partners. Girls may be betrothed at any time between infancy and adulthood. If they have not been betrothed or if their betrothal is canceled at the initiative of their promise or with his consent, girls may choose a spouse. However, the parents of both partners must approve of and consent to the match.

While this revision indicates the extent to which the ideal model of marriage has been modified by the mission situation and the experience of contemporary behavior, this model is nevertheless regarded, at least by adults, as the model of lawful behavior.

That adults expect to have a say in the marriages of adolescent girls is indicated by their frequent attempts to arrange girls' marriages. Adults, particularly mothers, had attempted to affect the marriage destinies of at least twenty-two of the fifty-five adolescent girls in the sample. They did so by betrothing the girls when they were young, by attempting to arrange matches for them when they were nubile, by witholding consent from matches proposed by the girls, or by refusing offers, or demands, made for them. All but one of these twenty-two cases involved older adolescent girls, that is, the thirty-nine girls between the ages of fourteen and twenty in 1981. Thus in at least 54 percent of these cases, mothers or other adults had attempted at least to influence girls' marriage choices.

These attempts, however, were not always effective; girls did not necessarily accept adult efforts on their behalf. Of the eighteen young girls known to have been betrothed, only one had married her promise by 1981. Marriage to the betrothed might still take place for five of these girls, those, for example, who were too young to marry in 1981. But for the remaining twelve girls, marriage to their betrothed seems unlikely. Four of these girls had married someone else, others had refused to marry their promises, and still others had been released by the men. In the latter cases, men had renounced their rights to a girl, either because they were already married to another woman or because they did not want the girl. For example, it was said that one man renounced his right to a girl because "she goes for anybody," that is, she was promiscuous (see also Hamilton 1981, 18).

Five girls were the objects of adult efforts to place them with a husband once they were nubile. (One girl's parents tried to give her to a second man after her promise had renounced his right to her.) In all of these cases the efforts failed because the match was vetoed by the girl, the proposed husband, or his parents. Two of these girls subsequently married other men; one chose an incorrect partner, the other married a man approved by her mother and father. A third had a child by a "straight" partner but her mother forbade a marriage between them. The fourth was said to be "running about" with boys, and the fifth was having an affair with a young boy of her own moiety at the time of this study.

By the end of 1981, fifteen of the adolescent girls had married, at least nine of them to a man of their choice, and in five of these cases the union was labeled "not straight."

THE PRESENT: MARGUERITE, NORA, AND KAY

Once, at least according to theory, the Aboriginal girls of Mangrove were betrothed before they were born and married before they reached sexual maturity. In 1981, however, marriage was far from the near-automatic event it had once ideally been. Take for example, the cases of Marguerite, Nora, and Kay.

At least a year prior to this study, Marguerite had acquired her first boyfriend, Brian; they had begun spending time together when they were in school. Brian had wanted Marguerite to run away with him, but Lily had put a stop to it. She did not want her daughter to have a "single baby." Marguerite and Brian were not correct marriage partners. Furthermore, Marguerite had been betrothed to Hamilton, the twenty-eight-year-old brother of the husband of her elder sister Hetty. Actually, Marguerite had originally been bestowed upon her sister's husband by her maternal grandmother when she was a "little girl," and her elder sister had been bestowed upon his older brother. But by the time Hetty was of marriage age, her promise had married another, so Hetty was given to the next son and Marguerite reserved for his younger brother. Marguerite, however, had refused to marry Hamilton. Lily had accepted this refusal; she would not "force" her daughter to marry, but she would not give permission for Marguerite to marry any other man, including Brian. Goodman had backed his wife's decision. By the end of the field period, Marguerite and Brian were no longer seeing each other and Brian was paying attention to another young girl named Ginny.

Kay had also been promised in marriage—to a man named Robin. This was arranged some years previously, when her elder sister, then a "little girl," was promised to Robin's older brother. In 1972, when Kay was nine, her sister and her promise were married. The boy's younger sister was intended as square back for Kay's elder brother; in 1976, however, she married another man. Before Kay's father died, he vowed, apparently in retaliation for this breach of contract and lack of promised reciprocity, that Kay would remain unmarried because her brother had been abandoned by his betrothed. Kay said that she would like to marry Robin; he was a young boy, just a few years older than she was. Her mother had said it was up to her to decide, but she said she was reluctant to marry because her sister-in-law had left her brother and he had no wife.

In 1976, when Nora was a "little girl," of eleven, one of her elder brothers sought to marry his present wife. As part of the negotiations for this marriage, Rosalind and her family promised that Nora would marry her brother's wife's younger brother Aaron when she was of the age to do so. When Nora was thirteen, however, she began seeing other men, including Aaron's clan brother, Tyler. At this time Rosalind took Nora to an outstation and gave her to the twenty-six-year-old Aaron, who was living there at the time, in an attempt to forestall the "mess" that

Nora was making. Her behavior had already contributed to a "big fight" on the settlement (Burbank 1980, 34). Nora joined her husband at the outstation, but not for long. Shortly afterward, a number of young girls were sent to the outstation as "punishment" for running around with men. When the girls ran away from the outstation, Nora joined them. Back at Mangrove, Nora began to see Tyler. When she did, Rosalind or another senior family member would give Nora a "hiding." Aaron would also "belt" her for running off with Tyler. But at some point during this period, Aaron released Nora from the marriage. It was also during this period that Nora's pregnancy was discovered. Rosalind watched her daughter lose weight in spite of all the meat she was eating, then noted a change in her complexion, and finally asked her daughter:

■ *"You pregnant?"*
"Yes," responded Nora.
"For who?"
"Tyler."

Even knowing of her daughter's condition, Rosalind advised her to "stay single." But Nora ignored this advice and her marriage to Tyler was consented to and recognized. This marriage, however, was of short duration.

Just two months before Nora's daughter, Leni, was born, another young girl, Claire, had given birth to a baby boy. Tyler, named as the father, denied it. But as the baby grew, Tyler decided that the boy's face was like his own.[15] He claimed the baby as his son and ran off with Claire, claiming her as his wife. Her guardian and father's sister at first refused to consent to the marriage. Tyler and Nora had separated by this time, but Claire's "auntie" was still "worried" about his first marriage. She may also have been concerned that Claire and Tyler were not regarded as correct marriage partners. Eventually, however, she gave in and, together with Claire's father, consented to the match. Their consent made it official, and the community worker noted it in her records. She also noted that Nora was now a single mother and made arrangements for her to receive Supporting Parents Benefit.

Marriage at Mangrove is not regarded as an arrangement to

be left to adolescents like Marguerite, Kay, and Nora. Like others, the marriage histories of each of the three young girls had been affected by decisions and actions taken by parents or grandparents. All three girls had been bestowed by others. Marguerite and Kay were prevented from marrying by others, and had Nora been less persistent, she might have been as well.

DISCUSSION

Marriage, the event that marks the beginning of a young girl's passage to adulthood, was not an automatic event at Mangrove in 1981. The three young girls, Marguerite, Nora, and Kay, were representative of their peers in this respect. Although each had been promised at some point in her life and each had considered marriage, none was married at the time of this study.

As noted in chapter 2, the promise system of the past did not always guarantee that marriage arrangements would go smoothly. For example, bestowers might promise a girl to more than one man, a young woman might be stolen, or a young couple might elope, leaving the young woman's betrothed wifeless (see, for example, Hiatt 1965, 84–85, 87–89; Shapiro 1981, 69–71; Warner 1969, 65–66, 71–78). At Mangrove, however, today's marriage arrangements have been further complicated by the period of maidenhood. The single status of nubile adolescents like Marguerite, Nora, and Kay and the number of incorrect marriages made by their peers indicate the extent to which problems have beset the institution of marriage in this Aboriginal community. In particular, the process of marriage is plagued by the extent to which adult expectations clash with adolescent desires—the topic of the next chapter.

The expectations of adults appear to be based on an amalgam of experience of marriages past and present. This experience includes what seems to have been a fairly recent sequence of change in betrothal form consisting of three overlapping stages: mother-in-law bestowal, wife bestowal, and choice of marriage partner with parental approval (see also Shapiro 1981). The fact that the apparent impetus for much of this change came from an imposed culture that was either ignorant or adverse to basic principles of Aboriginal social organization would seem to account for the existence of behavior that is regarded as wrong by many Aboriginal people. However, these changes are clearly embraced by some members of the population: generally the young unmarried adolescents.

■ 4

Contemporary Marriage: The Adolescent Perspective

The historical and cultural factors that form much of the basis of parental expectations about marriage today were presented in the last chapter. It is, however, apparent that many of Mangrove's young girls act on the basis of a different set of expectations. It is also apparent that this behavior frequently leads to conflict between adolescents and adults. This chapter completes the discussion of factors that contribute to conflict over marriage. In it I present adolescent expectations about male/female relationships and describe the strategies employed by adolescents and adults in the intergenerational battle over marriage.

JANE'S DILEMMA

As a means of discovering just what adolescent expectations might be, I composed the following story based on marriage histories of Mangrove's female population and on statements about ideal behavior in marriage contracts:

> When Jane was a little girl her mother promised her to Bert. All the time that Jane has been growing up Bert has been giving Jane and her mother dugong, fish, money,

clothes, and other nice things. Now Jane is big and her mother is saying she should marry Bert. But at school Jane met Sam. She likes him very much and he is straight for her. She would like to marry Sam. If you were Jane what would you do? Why?

I used this dilemma as a means of eliciting information, expectations, and attitudes about past and present marriage arrangements. The series of eight or nine questions that followed its presentation were designed with this purpose in mind.[1]

Marguerite, Kay, and Nora were presented with this dilemma. They were interviewed separately and asked to respond verbally after I read the story. I took notes of their answers while they talked.

It is not surprising, if one recalls the actual marriage histories of Nora and Marguerite, to find that they both answered that if they were Jane they would marry Sam. Marguerite chose him because "he's a nice-looking man and he is straight," Nora because he was her "boyfriend in school" and they "love each other very much." Both girls also expressed antipathy for Bert. Nora was particularly vehement in her dislike of Jane's promise. "He is an angry man and wild and he hit us for nothing." she comments. "I don't love him. He was so nasty to me. . . . I don't like him because he's so old, because he is a stinky man."

As Nora resolved Jane's dilemma, Jane's mother consents to her match with Sam and they "sit happy now, all of their lives," living together and "laughing at each other." ("Laugh" in Kriol and in Aboriginal English means both laugh and smile. For the people of Mangrove, both laughing and smiling at a member of the opposite sex indicate attraction.) Sam provides Jane and her mother with food and "lots of money." Some day he might become a "big boss," a councilor, town clerk, or office worker.

In Marguerite's response there is more conflict and, I think it fair to say, more realism. Jane does not want to marry Bert because she likes Sam "the best" as he is her age. Her mother tells Jane to stop going out with Sam and tries to "tempt" her to marry Bert, telling her to sit and walk with him. She also tells Bert "to fight with Sam" if Jane continues to see him. Jane, however, refuses to marry Bert. She sends word to him that if "he keeps on going like that, wanting to marry me, I'll run away with Sam." Jane's uncle tells Jane to marry Bert and threatens to "belt" her if she does not comply. Marguerite said that he might also take her and Bert out to the bush and leave them along together there. Recall that telling a girl to talk and walk with her betrothed is a recognized means of accustoming a girl to her future husband, while arranging for a couple to be alone together in the bush is an accepted technique for marrying off a girl who refuses to join her assigned husband.

In contrast to Marguerite and Nora, Kay said that if she were Jane she would marry Bert, "Cause that's the Law, to keep the Law. It should never be broken." Kay thought Bert would be "loyal" to Jane and a "good husband." He would work for her when she was sick and look after the kids. She did, however, suggest why Jane might prefer Sam: "Cause she's already been . . . seeing Sam a lot more than Bert when she was in school, alone together in the bush. That's why she wants to marry Sam." She also suggested that Jane might be "frightened" of Bert: "She'll be scared cause she'll think, 'Will he be rough or easy or will he lock her up in the house, like some men do, and be bossy?' . . . Maybe she'll think he got a girlfriend. Maybe when she's used to him after they have slept and are going together OK, the old girlfriend might tease her and they might run away *mangumangu* [elope]." Note that "tease" in Aboriginal English denotes a more hurtful action than it does in American English. It refers to either a verbal or physical attack and lacks all connotations of playfulness.

Right after making this statement, Kay expressed similar concerns about the kind of relationship she might have with her own husband: "Maybe we'll fight, maybe he'll trick me. If I go on a course maybe he'll play around with an old girlfriend. Or maybe he'll be jealous, be jealous of me thinking about the past and what I did when I was a young girl. And when we go to [a settlement], maybe he'll know how to drink and get drunk and belt me up thinking about the past."[2]

These three resolutions of Jane's dilemma suggest that at least some adolescents consider a number of factors when thinking about a future husband. They may think about his physical appearance, age, and economic potential. They may think about whether or not he is straight for them or if he is their promise. They may also consider certain character or personality traits such as aggressiveness, helpfulness, and fidelity. They may also take into account their own feelings about a man—whether or not they "like," "love," or are "used to" him.

I also read Jane's dilemma to five adult women, including Lily and Rosalind—the mothers of Marguerite and Nora, and Kay's mother's sister, Majiwi. Four of these women were married, with several children each. All were mothers or caretakers of girls in adolescence or just on the brink of adolescence. This group over-represents Christians and excludes the oldest and probably most tradition-oriented women in the community. However, with the exception of Majiwi who occupied a fairly unusual status as an unmarried adult woman, it seems typical of other mothers of adolescent girls in terms of age, schooling, language, and marriage histories.

Initially, it may appear surprising that of this group of adults only Lily and one other married woman answered that if they were Jane they would marry Bert. However, when their responses are examined in light of their own marriage histories, their replies are no more surprising than those of Marguerite and Nora. Rosalind, for example, justified her choice of Sam in nearly the same words she used to tell me of her own marriage, but with a difference:

> Maybe that first one never touched me, I never met him when I was in school. I met a friend and we talked and sat together so I'm used to that man. So when my promise comes, I'm going to say, "No, I don't like you." He says, "I'm your promise. When I call you come." But still I'm gonna say, "No. I don't like you." My mother is gonna try her best, telling me to go with that first one. But still I'm gonna say no, because I've grown big now and I have sense.

In her answer to this hypothetical dilemma, Rosalind would seem to be living her own life over more to her liking. It also seems consistent with Majiwi's single status that she would choose what may be regarded as the modern alternative. The other married woman who chose Sam had, in fact, chosen a "Sam" in real life, running off with her future husband and eventually marrying him in spite of maternal opposition.

The reasons given by these adult women for choosing Sam are quite similar to those given by the three young girls. All three who chose Sam justified their choice on the grounds that "Jane is really in love with him." Rosalind and the other married woman also mentioned Sam's fidelity: "Sam was always true to her and he didn't have any other girlfriends." Rosalind also raised the issue of relative age: "I'm going to be frightened because [Bert's] a grown man and I'm only young. [Sam's] gonna be my size, we gonna be in school together." She also pointed out that Jane was "used to" Sam, but not to Bert. As one of the two adults to choose Bert, Lily had little to say about Jane's reasons for wanting to marry Sam. The other married woman to choose Bert for Jane, did, however, suggest why Jane might prefer Sam: "Because they were good to each other. Sometimes her promise gives her a hiding. That's why she don't like him. She likes the other man, he's good to her. The first one might be jealous and bash her up."

The dilemma was also read to fourteen schoolgirls. This sample consists of the schoolgirls who attended class on the days the dilemmas were given. Six, or slightly over half of the fifth and sixth grade girls, were respondents. These girls were twelve and thirteen in 1981. This group seems representative of all but the two chronic truants of the class. Eight, or slightly over half, of the postprimary girls were respondents. These girls were between the ages of thirteen and sixteen in 1981. This group is, perhaps, less representative than it might be. All but one of the girls staying out of school at the time the dilemma was given were reported to have been involved in sexual liaisons and consequent conflicts with adults, whereas only four of the girls who attended class that day were likely to have had sexual experience, and only two were reported to have been involved in conflicts as a consequence. The dilemma was read to groups of two to five girls by their teachers in the classroom. They were asked to respond in writing and told that I would be given their answers to help me with the "book" I was writing about "young girls" at Mangrove. The school girls were asked only two questions: "If you were Jane, what would you do and why?" and "If you were Jane's mother, what would you do and why?"

Two of the younger schoolgirls, a twelve-year-old and a thirteen-year-old, chose to marry Bert. Four others chose to marry Sam. The general tenor of the reasons offered by this latter group may be summed up by the reply of Kay's twelve-year-old sister: Bert was "so ugly," Sam was "straight," and Jane loved Sam.[3] The remaining eight schoolgirls gave answers that seemed to remove Jane from the dilemma. One schoolgirl said that if she were Jane she would not have a boyfriend in the first place. Another, Marguerite's fourteen-year-old sister, said she would marry neither Sam nor Bert, and four others said they would remain "single." One schoolgirl said she would not marry Bert, and another said she would not marry Sam. The implications of these kinds of responses, which vary from those given by adults and the three young girls who answered verbally, are discussed in the next section.

FALLING IN LOVE

Love is a word that is, perhaps, coming to encapsulate the wishes, though not necessarily the expectations, of Mangrove's adolescent girls in the domain of male/female relationships. What do the people of Mangrove mean when they use the word *love*? A few examples of usage indicate that their meaning is not unlike our own. Rosalind, for example, explains the kind of relationship that results when a boy and a girl get to know each other at an early age:

> If they are gonna fall in love when they are small, nobody will stop them because they've been touching each other, having a date, like everyday. They see each other and they go somewhere and they can sit and talk. That girl's love and that boy's love will never end.

Here the postprimary girls' teaching assistant, an Aboriginal woman in her thirties, explains one of the things that can make young people "sad" or "sorry":

> When you see them upset and looking so miserable, maybe that girl and boy don't love each other and they get upset.

They were loving before and then they stopped. Maybe the boy doesn't like the girl and goes and finds another.

And here Nora discusses Jane's dilemma:

And maybe Jane's mother was sorry about Bert, telling Jane, "You have to marry Bert." But Jane said, "I don't love him. He was so nasty to me." And her mother will get very cross and chase Jane, but Jane doesn't love him.

And as a last example, a bit of graffiti:

Noah loves Suzette. Only for bloody sure. Till both have a kid and till both married for sure.

"Falling in love" was said to be the way some girls at Mangrove find themselves a husband. I asked the eight verbal respondents to Jane's dilemma how girls without promises got husbands. They all answered in more or less the same vein, "They gotta find their own." And how does a girl find one? Marguerite explained:

▪ *By finding herself a boyfriend.*
  But how does a girl do that?
  By going for a date every night and when she has that baby she'll go marry him.

A "date" at Mangrove is not quite the event it is for teenagers in Boston or Cleveland or Los Angeles. The word *date*, which has, to my knowledge, no equivalent in the Aboriginal language spoken at Mangrove, is generally used to refer to sexual intercourse. For example: "When a girl has a date with a boy she tells her best girlfriend that she saw his penis and how big it is and what kind of movement he makes. And the other girls go and try and ask him for a date. They want to see him, see his penis, and see what moves he makes." It is generally understood that a girl who has a date with a boy has sexual intercourse with him.

When discussing Jane's dilemma, Kay, Nora, Marguerite, and four of the five adult women considered whether or not

Jane was "used to" either Bert or Sam. A major component of being used to a man is sexual familiarity: "she's not used to him now. She's used to the other man, they meet and sleep together [have sexual intercourse]. That's why Jane wants to marry Sam."

In opposition to being used to a man, one is "frightened" of a man. On my first field trip to Mangrove, when my attention was focused on aggressive behavior (Burbank 1980), I asked eight female informants if women were "frightened" of men. The word had been used to describe people's state upon seeing such things as snakes, spears, and fights. The responses surprised me, thinking as I was of women as potential victims of male aggression. All eight women answered in the affirmative, but six of them were clearly speaking about women's "fear" of male sexuality. For example, Lily responded: "Some are. When I was a young girl, starting to have breasts, I was frightened of that old man, my husband. I would go to him and get fish, but I wouldn't sit beside him. I didn't like him. I didn't know men before, I didn't have sense. I was frightened." Here "know" is used in the biblical sense of the word, as it often is in Aboriginal English and Kriol. Note that part of having "sense" is "knowing" men.

Rosalind also answered my question in 1978. Her answer tells more about being frightened and being used to a man:

If you are not used to a man and he is going to make friend with you, if you never saw or talked with him before and he says, "I'm going to make you friend," your heart feels shaky and you are frightened and you can't go near him. When he comes close to you, you can't talk much, you are frightened, shy. But when you know him from the time you were little, then you can't be frightened because you have talked from that time and know each other. Then you won't be frightened. But the man you don't see or talk to, then you are going to be frightened, feel shy.

Note that in the context of this statement "friend" means "lover." It is commonly used in this sense in the Aboriginal English of Mangrove.

Being used to a man is viewed as an advantage in the marriage process and was the stated objective of women's strategies for acquainting little girls with the men they would eventually marry. But being used to a man can be a real detriment to the marriage process and to a stable marriage, if a girl becomes used to the wrong man. Again Rosalind speaks: "When a girl is young and never knew a man and she makes a friend and they are friends for a long time, the girl won't leave that man if another man tries to get her, or her parents try and stop her, because she has too much sweat from that man. She will love only him. That man's sweat can grow up that girl, she will love only him." The sweat referred to here is that which comes from the activity of sexual intercourse.

Lest it be thought that the issue of premarital sex is one that touches only the three central characters of this description and their families, a look at a few figures is in order. There is evidence that at least thirty of the fifty-five young girls at Mangrove in 1981 had engaged in premarital intercourse on at least one occasion. This evidence includes self-report, reports of "dating" that I judge reliable, and records of pregnancy, miscarriage, and out-of-wedlock birth. In only one of the known cases was a girl's partner her betrothed. In eight cases, however, girls were known to have married one of their premarital partners.

FEMALE ADOLESCENT EXPECTATIONS ABOUT MEN AND MARRIAGE

It is apparent that adults equate love and sex with marriage. That is, girls' sexual behavior, whether it is actually motivated by a desire to find a husband or by boredom, loneliness, or curiosity—all suggested but unexplored motivations—is perceived by the adult community as a threat to the system. From the adults' perspective it may lead through pregnancy or habituation to an incorrect marriage. But do adolescent girls equate love, sex, and marriage as adults seem to, at least when they are thinking about adolescent behavior?

The adolescent girls of Mangrove have during their lifetimes been exposed to many of the same examples of romantic love as Western adolescents. They see Hollywood movies, listen to popular music, and even watched Lady Di's wedding on the school video machine. And, like Western adolescents, the ado-

lescent girls of Mangrove have before their eyes daily examples
of what happens after the honeymoon is over. Might not the
fact that a number of schoolgirls chose to remain unmarried
when confronted with Jane's dilemma suggest that marriage is
perceived, at least by some, as a less than desirable situation?
Listen to the reply of two fourteen-year-olds to my question,
"When are girls ready to marry?":

> When they are young, when they leave school, that's the
> time they get married. [Like] Nora. They bear a baby and
> the father leaves the girl and goes to another girl, tricking.
> He goes two ways, to a girl and to another girl. Some do like
> that, especially these young boys. When they follow their
> husband he chases them back home and she gets a hiding
> and a baby.

In the middle of this answer and its immediate association to
Nora's marital history one of the girls interjected, "I feel sorry."
Sorrow does not seem like an emotion that would lead to a de-
sire to imitate.

Kay, for one, is conscious of the effect that the example of
others has on her thinking. She put it thus: "Like you get a picture. . . . Maybe I'll see some couple have a fight, maybe this
picture will happen to me."

Marguerite was certainly aware of young girls who had
been mistreated by their husbands. Here, for example, she discusses the abandonment of two young girls by their husbands:

> Ella should have stayed [single] like me. But she wanted to
> marry Andy. But he left her. He is at [another settlement]. I
> don't know what she's gonna do. . . . Poor Ella is here wan-
> dering around. . . . Maybe he is only leaving her because
> she is pregnant. He is acting like Violet's husband. He left
> Violet for a long time when she was pregnant. Violet didn't
> like him when he came back from [another settlement];
> she used to hate him. He used to come and talk to me,
> "That Violet hates me." . . . [She hates him] because he left
> her alone.[4]

For reasons that will become clearer later in this chapter,
Marguerite's thoughts on men and marriage at the time of the

study were as likely formed by her own experience with Brian as by the fortunes of other young girls. Nevertheless, Nora's example seems to have had some impact upon her perception of men and marriage—possibly as confirmation of her experience of male perfidy: "Marriage is no good. To be married to a young man is no good. The girls don't like to be married because the young man might trick you, like when you have a baby with a young man . . . like Nora. Like she got that baby from Tyler and married him, but she is having a hard time with her husband. He is tricking her all the time with Claire." Marguerite made a similar statement to her rival, Ginny: "You will find a baby and then [your boyfriend] will not like you anymore and just get another girl. Like happened to Nora."

Abandonment, of a sort, is not an entirely new experience for Mangrove's female population. As mentioned in chapter 3, a man's acquisition of a new wife might lead to a physical separation from his former spouse or spouses, with the more senior wives living apart from the marital household. Such was the case, for example, for three women between the ages of fifty-five and sixty in 1978. These women, however, are not regarded as "separated" or "divorced" (terms that seem just to be coming into use). It is expected that they will continue to receive support from their husbands and, in fact, may continue sociable relations with them (Burbank 1980, 107). But recently, in 1978 and 1981, two marriages other than Nora's ended in separations that were regarded as permanent. In both cases, the wives seemed to have had as much to do with the separations as the husbands. In both it was reported that the couples were "cut out all together" because they were "fighting too much." All involved were relatively young; the men were twenty-two and twenty-six, the women nineteen and twenty-eight at the time of the separations. There were no children in either union.

Nor is a lack of male fidelity an entirely new experience for Mangrove's female population. A discussion of male adultery at Mangrove is somewhat confounded by the possibility of polygynous marriage, for male extramarital sex may be just a first step in the legitimate acquisition of a new wife (see also Shapiro 1981, 70–71). However, as has been mentioned, the females of Mangrove have, in recent years, come to expect their marriages to be monogamous. A man's extramarital affairs are viewed, at least by some in the female half of the population, as "tricking." In this domain of male/female relations, however, women may be giving nearly as good as they get. Instances of adultery at Mangrove are, at least for the outsider, indicated by fights over adultery. In 1977 and 1978, seven such fights came to my attention. Two of these fights were between married couples; one over the husband's purported behavior, the other over the wife's. In the five other fights the injured parties fought with their spouses' paramours. Three of these fights were between men and two between women (Burbank 1980, 87, 91; see also Goodale 1971, 130–133; Hart and Pilling 1960, 80–83; Hiatt 1965, 107–112; Meggitt 1962, 97–99; Warner 1937, 70, 73–75).

A number of young girls have had firsthand experience with male infidelity, not as betrayed wives but as girlfriends of married men. "Do girls have any enemies?" I once asked Marguerite: "Only married ladies. Young girls have married ladies for enemies because all the time they are talking about them. Sometimes married ladies get jealous of their husbands because they are walking around and all of the young girls walk around too. And they might meet each other some place." Kay also mentioned that "girls get jealous of their husbands and blame it on young girls, especially when they see them walking around with the young girls." Apparently, this jealousy is not entirely unfounded. In 1981 at least three of the young girls were reportedly involved with married men. In the previous year, one adolescent was impregnated by her married partner, and Marguerite's rival, Ginny, had run off with a married man. Claire, of course, and Tyler had been carrying on more or less throughout his marriage to Nora. Nevertheless, or perhaps because, young girls have had so much experience of male infidelity, either directly from firsthand experience or indirectly from the experience of their friends and peers, it forms at least a part of their expectations about men and marriage. Two of the three girls spoke directly of their concerns about male fidelity; the third, Nora, clearly suffered from a lack of it in her marriage.

But comments about Nora's marriage indicate that what may concern young girls the most is not male infidelity per se, but rather the abandonment to which it may lead. Rosalind's tale of a fight over Ginny's affair with a married man (mentioned earlier) suggests this concern may be widespread in the female community:

> Wyatt left Patti and was running around with Ginny. One day at the shop Patti went after that girl and there was a big fight. They fought: wrestling, and after that with fighting sticks. When they were wrestling they tore each other's dresses off and they were fighting in pants. You could see their bodies, everything. All the little children were watching. Then [Patti's elder sister] took partner for Patti and [Ginny's elder sister] took partner for Ginny. Two sisters together fighting. And they fought and broke each other's dresses too. . . . [After the fight they said], "Patti is right for fighting for her husband." and "She didn't like that other woman taking her husband away from her." And they said to Wyatt, "Why don't you stay with your wife and kid, you got no right to go to that other woman, you should stay and look after that wife and kid."

Men, if not marriage, seem to occupy many of the thoughts of Mangrove's young girls. For example, as a part of the school's "work experience" program, I gave a talk to the postprimary class on what an anthropologist does and then held several other sessions with a small group of girls. For our last session the girls chose classmates as informants and asked them one or two questions. The question they chose to ask: "Who is your boyfriend?" I found, however, that these were not topics to be approached directly. Nevertheless, the three young girls talked to me, in varying degrees, about men and marriage. Occasionally they volunteered a personal experience, attitude, or feeling; more often they answered, in a more impersonal vein, questions I tried to phrase in general terms and put as nonintrusively as possible.

Speaking in general terms, Marguerite presented men as an important part of young girls' lives. "What," I asked her after we had been working together for about a month, "makes young girls happy?":

> When she sees her boyfriend and when her boyfriend asks her for a date. And she might say yes, and she goes and she sees her girlfriends around and tells them to take her to

that boy. . . . That's one of the main things that makes all the girls happy.

"And what," I then asked, "makes young girls sorry or sad?":

For a girl, if the young boy refuses and says no to the girl who asked him for a date, and the young girl feels very sad and a bit upset and she goes laughing or sulking or teasing . . . that young boy who said no.

Relationship with boys were also the topics of her answers to my questions about things that make young girls "angry" and "shame." According to Marguerite, girls get "angry" when their boyfriends have "a date with another girl." They are "shame" when their parents "growl" at them for "running away" with young boys.

The four other young girls of whom I asked this series of questions also talked about boys. Here, for example, are Kay's and Nora's answers to the question about "shame":

Maybe a man got married to another girl and that young girl really loved him, that makes her shame. She won't ever cut across his pathway, she will never want to see him. She will be shy.

If they have a boyfriend and that boyfriend stares at them, it makes them get shame, or if the boyfriend growls at them it makes them feel shame and sad in their heart.

But these four girls also spoke of other things and other people. Two schoolgirls, a twelve-year-old and a fourteen-year-old, for example, said that boys and running off with boys made girls happy, but also singing and dancing. Thus Marguerite's exclusive focus on members of the opposite sex in her answers to the series of questions suggests that her preoccupation with men was somewhat greater than that of the other girls, at least at the time the questions were asked.

Marguerite also made statements about marriage that suggest she thought there could be strong emotional bonds between men and women. I presented her with a hypothetical dilemma in which a man must choose between stealing some medicine for his wife or letting her die.[5] Here is Marguerite's solution:

> He should [steal the medicine] because he don't want his wife to die from the terrible disease. If his wife dies he won't have any wife again and he'll feel upset and lonely without a wife. . . . If she dies and he sees one of the girl's family . . . they will make him think about her and he will feel sad and miserable and he'll think about going out to the club and buying some beer and make himself drunk so he will stop thinking about his wife. And the other thing, if he sees any man with their wife and kids, that'll make him think about his wife a lot and make him upset and worried, and make him think about his life and how it's gonna end up and maybe he'll kill himself by getting in an accident . . . [like a] car accident or by fighting another man so he, the other man, will stab him so he could die the same way as his wife.

But when asked more direct questions about men and marriage, Marguerite's replies were almost always negative, "Do you like young boys, or not like them?" I asked her. "Not like them," she replied, "because they are too stupid." "What does that mean?" "They think about lots of women, lots of women, and because they throw stones, break louvres in the office, and break in the school and the shop." A question about boys that show off elicited this answer:

> I hate them. I don't like boys very well . . . because they show off all the time. . . . When that man got another girl and that [first] girl for him don't know he got another and he shows off a lot and his girlfriend gets to know who his other girlfriend is and she gets a bit mad with him and he goes stealing trucks and breaking in, doing silly things, that young boy. . . . [He shows off to a girl] by talking to her and chasing her and giving her just a little action [hand signs] to tell her where to go, to hide from his girlfriend so his girlfriend won't see him talking to the other girl.[6]

This discussion about boys who show off suggests that Brian's defection to Ginny at least contributed to the negative attitude about men that Marguerite displayed at the time of the study. A story she made up about the day of a young boy leads to a similar conclusion:

> There was a young boy. He wasn't working, he was a bludger.[7] He was walking around and didn't know what to do or how to get a job. He was out of school for a long time and he had a girlfriend and his girlfriend didn't know how to get a job either. They both bludged. They always fight and argue over [other] girls and boys. They are not right line [straight] for each other. They are wrong side. If only the mother of the boy knew about the girl making friends with him she would have gotten a hiding a long time ago. They are nearly going to have a kid but the mothers of the boy and the girl don't know about it.[8] But all the people around the community know about those two making friends. Those two already follow each other everywhere. But the people just hate the girl following the boy all the time. Sometimes when she sees the boy's old girlfriend she just spies on her or follows him so that he can't make eyes at his old girlfriend anymore. All the time she does that.

Marguerite's response to a direct question about marriage was also negative. "What kind of a man would you like to marry?": "I don't like men. I am sick of men. . . . I don't like them. . . . [No matter] how much they can talk and laugh at me, I can't take any notice. Even when men want to marry me I always tell them off. 'I don't like you. You know why? Because I am sick [of men]. I don't like you.'" Only in fantasy did Marguerite say that she would like to be married, and then only in order to have children. I once asked her, "If a wizard could make you anything, what would you like to be?" "A fine lady," she responded, then added: "I could be a princess. I could ride on horses and I could wear those big dresses. I could marry a prince, another king's son, so I could have kids and be happy with the kids." But a negative attitude about men and marriage was again evident in her answer to my very next question, "What would you like to be when you are a proper woman?":

■ *I can stay single and I don't like to marry a man. I think they are too silly. And can't control themselves if they marry a woman and they'll get jealous all the time and give her a hiding all the time. . . . I don't like that sort of a man.*

It's better if I stay single instead of marrying a man that can't control himself.

What if you could find a man who could control himself?

I can make friend with him but I can't marry him cause I don't trust men. They can make friend with you and make you pregnant and go to another girl.

Perhaps her most emphatic statement on the subject was, "I won't get married. Those two [my mother and father] say I'll stay single. I hate men! They boss you and they find other women and they trick you. I won't do washing for any man!"

Kay, like Marguerite, had seen her peers unhappy in their marriages, but seemed to have more confidence in men than Marguerite. For example, she comforted Ella during her husband's absence: "when she was big [with child] she was worried about her husband, worried he wouldn't come back and the baby would have no father. And I had a good talk with her and told her not to worry, he would come back." On more than one occasion Kay also expressed a desire to get married. When I asked her what she would like to be when she was a "proper woman," she answered: "[If I could] find a husband it would be better for me. That's what a proper woman would be like. And I'd be good to that man's family and also to my own family. . . . Like cook food, do washing, clean the house. That would make me a proper woman." Kay also seemed to have positive expectations about male-female relationships:

A girl was made to be loved by a boy and a boy was made to be loved by a girl. That's the way God made them. Like Adam and Eve. Adam was lonely by himself with all these animals, so God put Eve in the Garden. Adam found her there and God told him Eve was there to be friend with him. So that's how it goes with women and men. Women and men should be perfect together and get along quite well as friends.

And yet, as detailed earlier in this chapter, Kay expressed some concerns about men and marriage. She knows that some men are unfaithful, that some men get jealous and drunk and beat their wives, and she is concerned lest this happen to her should she get married. Being single has its advantages. Here is Kay's comment after witnessing a fight between two young women over the affections of a young man: "That's why I like to stay single, so I won't let any man make me feel bad."

Nora also made positive statements about members of the opposite sex. She said she liked young boys "because they look pretty and nice. "She also liked boys who "walk together, talk together nice way, carry the baby and make it sleep with a bottle and sleep together the proper way, not leaving their wife." She too wanted to marry. When first presented with Jane's dilemma, Nora ignored the questions and made the following statement: "If I had a boyfriend maybe he'd give me money and clothes and some fish, maybe dugong. Maybe his mother would tell him to marry me. Maybe we would be married and go somewhere and stay for years, forever and ever. Maybe I would have a child for him. Maybe he would work and earn money, perhaps as a mechanic." When asked what she would like to be when she became a proper woman, Nora told me what she'd like to do: "carry a baby, wash the baby's clothes, cook damper for [my] husband and kids, make milk for the kids and maybe go out shopping." Like Marguerite and Kay, Nora seemed to have some positive wishes, if not expectations, about male/female relationships. She expressed what might be regarded as a romantic view of marriage when she imagined that Sam and Jane would "sit happy now, all of their lives."

But like Marguerite and Kay, Nora also indicated that her thoughts about men were not always positive. Bert, for example, when spurned by Jane, behaves aggressively in Nora's development of the dilemma: "Maybe he'll get wild at Jane and Jane's mother and maybe he'll get something, spear or rifle, and maybe shoot them. . . . Maybe [Jane's father] will go and chase Sam. . . . Maybe he will [strike] Sam in the leg and Jane will go crying to him and Bert will go laughing at her and teasing Sam."

But it is not just spurned suitors who aggress against women. Nora also talks about husbands who aggress against wives:

Mayabe [a young boy] will steal something from the shop in the night and go back with the food and if the young wife sees him walking with the tin [of food] and growls at him, "Where did you get that tin?" "I was stealing it from the shop." "Take it back." And maybe he will take it back and maybe he will shame and go back and belt her.

And Nora talks about husbands who leave their wives:

If that young boy leaves his wife and kid maybe [old people] feel sorry and [it] makes them sad or ugly faces. Or maybe they will growl, "Why did you leave your daughter and wife?" Maybe for nothing or just because he's sniffing petrol or he's got a new girlfriend.

I asked Nora if Billy Smith, Heinz's Aboriginal counterpart, should steal medicine for his wife if he did not "like" her any more. Her answer indicates the extent to which she can conceive of male hostility: "No. Because he doesn't love, like her. And maybe he'll get angry wild at her and tell her, 'I don't like you anymore. You can die anyway.' And maybe the lady will be sick enough and maybe dying." It is perhaps telling that Nora would create in this hypothetical situation this behavior from a man who once, according to Nora, loved his wife. However, Nora's conceptualization of Billy Smith's behavior does not differ greatly from those offered by Marguerite and Kay.[9]

In their apparent preoccupation with male fidelity and control of jealous and aggressive impulses, Marguerite, Kay, and Nora seem to share the concerns of their mothers' generation. Four of the five adult women answering questions about Jane's dilemma suggested that Bert, as a man frustrated in his wishes, would behave aggressively. For example, in the role of Bert, Kay's mother's sister, Majiwi, says: "I'd be angry and not [want] my promise to be taken by another guy. Lots of trouble. Unless I forgot about it and was quiet, not making trouble. But always there comes big trouble . . . fighting, arguing, even girls can be hit by that promise man."

As mentioned previously, male fidelity was also an issue with the adult respondents to Jane's dilemma. Three of the women suggested that Jane would not want to marry Bert because he was unfaithful to Jane: "He had so many girlfriends." Rosalind suggested that a genesis of female rejection of the promise system is male rejection of the promise: "[Some] boys don't like their promise. They go to another woman, young girl. If the boy gonna start first, tricking her, then the girl's gonna do exactly the same."

Adult women are also concerned with similar dimensions in the behavior of husbands. They, however, make a distinction between men as husbands that young girls do not seem to make—the difference between old men and young men (see also Cowlishaw 1979, 159–160, 192). A statement of Rosalind's sums up this distinction succinctly:

> On outstations young girls don't like to marry young men because they belt them and make them work. They make them wash and boil tea, bring water, wash his clothes, make his bed. But old men they like better. Because old men can't make them work. . . . And old men can't be jealous, they are just going to sit there. . . . Because a young man is jealous he will do this and that and give his wife a hard time. . . . "Oh you are going to those young men," just because they are sitting watching her as she goes by. He might hit or punch her.

Rosalind recognized, however, that young girls did not see things this way. She also said that there were negative consequences of girls' preference for young men as husbands: "They like young people, but it's very hard for them because young people are spoiled. They love each other when they are young, but when they have a kid that man can't love'm much. He's gonna keep away from her because he's gonna find another girl." Majiwi pointed out that a young man may not be a good provider. As a husband he may just "sit, not looking after mother and child. He just gambles and gets money from there, not looking after the child properly." She and Lily noted, like Rosalind, that young men are more likely to "leave and get a divorce."

INTERGENERATIONAL CONFLICT OVER MARRIAGE

While some adult women seem to share their adolescent daughters' perceptions of desirable and undesirable male qualities, such considerations have little place, at least ideally, in the selection of appropriate marriage partners.[10] Here the relevant criteria are basically whether partners are straight or promised. But if Kay, Nora, and Marguerite are representative of young girls at Mangrove today, the majority of adolescents can only be expected to marry men that they "love" or not marry at all if they find no one they want to marry. Freedom of choice is the issue in the intergenerational conflict over marriage, whether young girls are attempting to avoid an arranged marriage, marry a man of their choice, or avoid marriage altogether.

Some adults voiced an acceptance of free choice in marriage. For example, in 1978 Marguerite's mother Lily told me: "This time is different now, like European. We are thinking new ways. We are not promising our daughters. They are going to choose themselves." But this statement is misleading. Adult expectations are better reflected in another woman's promise to her daughters that they could choose their own husbands as long as they chose someone "straight." As mentioned in the previous chapter, mothers had taken some action to direct the marriages of the majority of girls between the ages of fourteen and twenty. Indigenous rules of partner selection and the expectation that parents should arrange, or consent to, marriages limit the choice. So, too, does the general expectation that all girls should marry.

Not all adolescent behavior remains within the confines set by adult expectations, however. Cases of physical and verbal aggression between adolescent girls and adults over marriage and related issues suggest, for example, that girls do not necessarily accept adult efforts to arrange their marriages. In 1978 I was aware of ten such cases of conflict (Burbank 1980, 194–195). In 1981, fifteen came to my attention.[11] The nine marriages of choice made by adolescents by 1981 also suggest that girls are not conforming to adult expectations.

Answers to Jane's dilemma also reflect the extent to which free choice in marriage is an issue, if not an expectation, of Mangrove's young girls. By far the majority of adolescent girls, twelve of seventeen, chose a course of action that does not lead to lawful marriage by adult standards. Six of the girls chose to marry Sam, the others to remain single or at least not to marry Bert. On the other hand, as the adults were more or less split between the traditional alternative and that chosen by most of the adolescents, one wonders at the source of adult motivation in this conflict. Why, for example, would Rosalind, who chose to marry Sam herself in the hypothetical situation, force her daughter Nora into marriage with a disliked promise in real life?

It seems reasonable to assume that adult women who had chosen to marry Sam in this hypothetical dilemma, or in their own lives, would be more in sympathy than conflict with daughters who chose to do likewise. Here it is informative to look at the answers to the second question, "If you were Jane's mother, what would you do?" These answers demonstrate that this assumption is not made by the majority of adults and many of the adolescents who responded to Jane's dilemma. Of the five adults, four said they would take Bert's side as Jane's mother, regardless of whether they chose as Jane to marry Sam or Bert. For example, although as Jane, Majiwi had chosen to marry Sam, as Jane's mother she said, "I would be strong and speak up and talk for him that gave me dugong and money." The fifth woman, Lily, in the role of Jane's mother tells her daughter to "stay single." She will not force her to marry Bert, but she will not allow her to marry Sam, just as she had in fact done with Marguerite: Lily did not force Marguerite to marry her promise, but she would not allow her to marry Brian. Six of the adolescent girls, including Kay and Marguerite, took Bert's side in the role of Jane's mother; the seventh, Nora, although she eventually allowed Jane to marry Sam, did so only after being "wild" with Jane and fighting with Sam's mother. (One schoolgirl did not respond to the second question. Three replies were not clear.)

These replies suggest that many respondents were thinking about social roles rather than their own preference when they answered the question. That is, a woman in the role of Jane, an adolescent girl with a boyfriend in school, would choose to marry Sam not so much as a preference as a prediction. She would assume that an adolescent such as Jane would choose to marry Sam. Similarly, an adolescent in the role of Jane's mother would tell her daughter to marry her promise, not because she would like her mother to act this way, but because she thinks her mother would act this way.

ADULT MOTIVATION IN CONFLICT OVER MARRIAGE

While freedom of choice is at stake for adolescent girls, other principles of social organization are at stake for their seniors in many of the current conflicts over marriage. As discussed in chapter 2, at least part of Aboriginal social identity is based on the correct juxtaposition of paternal and maternal statuses represented by a straight marriage. When a girl chooses an inappropriate partner the parental question is: "How are you gonna call the child? What's the [kin-class of the] child gonna be?"

It is thus not surprising to find that women bestowing their daughters in marriage are not expected to act outside or above the Law. A woman is not only responsible for the disposition of her daughter in marriage, she is held responsible for her disposition. It is a recognized possibility that a disappointed suitor may attack his potential mother-in-law. Here, for example, Nora anticipates Bert's behavior when Jane's mother allows her to marry Sam: "'You have to give me Jane because I've been looking after you. . . . But now you gave her to Sam.' And he gets cross at Jane's mother and maybe [strikes] her with a spear or an axe."

When it is time for a girl to be bestowed, women are expected to act in concert with their brothers and at least consult with other family members, such as their own mothers and fathers. These people may also be the targets of aggression if promises or rules are broken. Kay anticipates the consequences of the broken promise: "[Jane's uncles] get worried because Bert's family throws spears at them and Bert's mother comes and fights with Jane."

A woman may also be attacked by family members of the boy her daughter is dating, especially if the couple are not straight:

> If a young girl doesn't have a promise she's gonna choose until she finds [a man to marry]. If wrong way she's gonna have a hard problem. But if she chooses the right one, that's OK. But if she chooses the wrong one, the mother of the boy, if she hears what they are doing, she won't let that boy marry the girl. . . . They are gonna have an argument

or a fight. . . . The mother and father of the boy are gonna argue with the mother and father of the girl: "Tell your daughter to go right way."

It is understandable why women in their role as mothers defended the rules of the system. These women have been exposed to the sources of adolescent expectations, the mission and school teachings, the movies and popular songs that all—inadvertently or deliberately—present marriage as an individual affair, based on romantic love and choice of partner. They share adolescent expectations about mate selection insofar as they are able to predict the behavior of their children. But as adults, particularly as mothers held responsible for the behavior of their daughters, they act largely in terms of indigenous rules. One might predict that when girls such as Nora and Marguerite, who have chosen or tried to choose their own husbands, have daughters of marriageable age, they will attempt to marry their daughters off to appropriate partners.

ADULT STRATEGIES

The discussion in chapter 3 made it clear that conflict over marriage attended by disruption and resistance is not a new experience for the Aborigines of Mangrove. There are too many tales at Mangrove of past love affairs and elopements to think otherwise. However, the frequency, type, and success of resistance in 1981 may be a very recent development. Members of the senior generation are not facing an incomprehensible behavior when confronted by an adolescent girl who wants to marry a man of her choice. What may be more incomprehensible, however, are the choices that some girls are making—choices that do not seem to take into account their partner's kin classification or moiety affiliations.

Adolescence is perceived as the time of burgeoning sexuality. The budding breasts signaling that a little girl is now becoming a young girl also signal that she is approaching sexual maturity and may now be sexually active. According to the ideal of the past, by this time a girl should be securely ensconced in her marital household with a man she had been promised to from infancy if not before she was born. In 1981, however, this ideal was realized by no one. And it appears that the majority of Mangrove's mothers fail to marry off their daughters before they become sexually active. This period, rather than being a time when a mother can relax her efforts, is a time when a mother must begin, or renew, her efforts to see that her daughter is married correctly. In the ideal past, a little girl with little sense and little resolve was eased into marriage with her assigned husband. But by 1981, premenarcheal marriage was largely unfeasible; adults were attempting to direct more mature and experienced beings who had ideas for themselves and the capacity to carry them out. Thus it is not surprising that adolescence, this newly created period of maidenhood, is a period of time in which the junior and senior generations of Mangrove engage in a battle of wills, if not in actual battle.

In the absence of early marriage, parents have only their ability to persuade or coerce recalcitrant adolescents. Attempts of the latter sort are often public knoweldge, if not public acts, and as mentioned earlier, fifteen cases in which adolescent girls were the targets of adult aggression due to conflict over marriage and related issues came to my attention in 1981. In thirteen of these cases the girl's choice of an incorrect partner was clearly a matter of concern. Seven adolescent girls were the targets of aggression in these fifteen cases. They were "growled" at or given a "hiding" by one of their own parents or by one of the parents of the boy with whom they were "running about." One girl who was running around with a married man was stabbed in the leg by her father.

The man who stabbed his daughter was said to be an aggressive man, more so than most others. But while people's reactions suggest his action was regarded as excessive, it was not without precedent nor beyond the realm of expectation. For example, parents had been said to threaten their daughters with a stab in the foot or leg to keep them from running around with men. It was also reported that in 1980, a woman had hit her daughter's foot with this intent. This man claimed it was an accident—his daughter had stepped back into the spear he held as she was "wrestling" with her mother. Rosalind disagreed with this interpretation: "Last time when she ran off he said that if she ran off again he would [strike] her in the leg."

In this case, the Northern Territory police were called by Mangrove's Aboriginal police aid: the father was taken away and booked, and then returned to Mangrove to await trial. In most cases of physical discipline, for such aggression is so regarded, the police are not notified; according to a law enforcement agent who had spent several years working in the area, when cases of disciplinary-type aggression are reported, the police may turn a deaf ear. In most cases girls are not seriously injured. According to local clinic staff, the bruises they report with after a "hiding" are usually less severe then the contusions sustained by their mothers in fights over the behavior of their adolescent children.

Parents also employ less violent means of channeling their daughters' behavior. Withholding consent from a match that might otherwise be made is one such means. Forbidding marriage altogether, as Lily did with Marguerite, though less common, is another. Parents may also attempt to separate couples by sending their daughters, or sons, away from the community to live with relatives on another settlement. Like Rosalind, parents may also arrange for their daughters to begin living with their husbands. Or they may encourage their sons-in-law to claim their daughters as wives.

ADOLESCENT STRATEGIES

Adolescent girls, however, have developed what may be seen as counterstrategies to combat adult maneuvers in the intergenerational battle over marriage.

Adolescent disregard of adult standards is supported by the conditions of settlement life. Western ideology has fueled, if not instigated, the motive of choice; Western institutions offer the opportunity and the means for choosing. As I mentioned in chapter 2, on the settlement a large number of adolescents, likely many more than were coresidents in pre-mission times, have the opportunity for daily interaction in settings that did not exist in precontact times. Take, for example, the school. For five hours a day, five days a week, nine months out of the year, adolescent girls and boys mix in coeducational classrooms removed from the vicinity and supervision of most Aboriginal adults.

Though only a few hundred yards from the Aboriginal village, the extent to which the school is isolated from the community is indicated by the fact that at night it is a favored spot for adolescent liaisons and petrol sniffing.

The school also provides adolescent girls with a peer group. Classified by chronological age, girls and boys of thirteen years and up are grouped together in the postprimary classrooms. Such groups probably did not exist in pre-mission times because girls of this age were then most likely residing in the camps of their husbands and their elder co-wives, and boys were restricted to the bachelors' camp.

The support girls receive from their peers for a deviant course of action may be considerable and critical. For example, it was reported that when a group of three schoolgirls were presented with Jane's dilemma they first conferred: "Stay single?" and all three answered that if they were Jane they would "stay single." Such support may well make a difference for more than a written answer to a hypothetical question. For example, one older woman complained on many occasions that young girls refuse to join their promised husbands because their friends "tempt" them to "stay single."

Dating is also facilitated by peer group support. This activity is regarded as illegitimate by the adult community and must be pursued covertly. The extent to which contacts with eligible members of the opposite sex need to be hidden was underlined by Marguerite and Nora when I asked them if they preferred sitting and talking to young boys or young girls. Both answered "young girls," and both of their explanations included the wish to avoid the sorts of trouble that might follow if they were seen talking to young boys. Here is Marguerite's explanation:

> If we talk with boys some people might think we might be making friend with each other cause the people here think that way . . . old people, young people, married people. . . . [I wouldn't want anybody to see me talking to a boy] cause they might think silly way. They might talk about rubbish things. [That is, they might think it was a sexual relationship and gossip about it.]

Nora said the girl's parents might "chase" the boy if they saw him talking to their daughter.

Girls may rely on the assistance of their friends when it comes to dates. From among the peer group a "mailman" may be recruited to carry the verbal message or letters that announce desire and fix assignations.[12] Not only may friends act as go-betweens, setting up the time and place, but they may also serve as camouflage. Marguerite tells a story that illustrates the importance of girlfriends in the pursuit of boyfriends:

> There is a schoolgirl who sleeps a lot and sometimes wakes up late for school. . . . Sometimes she goes to school after [morning tea]. The teacher sometimes feels a little bit angry and asks questions about where she stays every night. . . . [After school] she goes playing at the sand hills with her friends till it comes nighttime. She never goes home. Some of her friends go home but she likes to stay all the time at the hill and watch for her boyfriend to come and stay up all night. So the next time she won't come to school early. She'll come late. Her mother thinks she is with her friends, but she isn't. She always stays with her boyfriend.

On at least one occasion the adolescent peer group assisted a liaison that was more than just a date. This was in the case of a young woman who eloped with an unpromised partner just a few years prior to this study. As the account goes, the young man went to the airstrip to wait for the plane. A little later the informant noticed a group of young girls, including the future bride, walking down the road from the village in the direction of the airstrip. At the airstrip this young girl joined her future husband and flew with him to another settlement. They returned to Mangrove after the furor caused by their elopement had died down. The girl's mother quarreled with them, but they were allowed to stay married. It is as suspect for a woman to walk out of the village alone as it is for her to be seen alone with a man; the immediate assumption is that she is going off to meet a lover. On the other hand, a group of females is not regarded with suspicion. They may be going out fishing or gathering or for some other legitimate purpose. The company of her peers on her walk to the airstrip was essential for the success of this young girl's venture. So, too, may the company of her peers enable a young girl to meet her boyfriend on the outskirts of the village.

Peer support of deviant behavior may be emotional or psychological as well as practical. When presenting Jane's dilemma I asked if Jane would talk to someone if she did not know what to do. Nora responded in the following fashion: "Yes. Maybe I'll say to some girlfriend of mine, 'I don't want Bert. I want Sam.' . . . Maybe she'll say, 'Yes, you gonna marry Sam. We don't like Bert because he is an angry man and wild and he hit us for nothing.' 'Sure,' I will say. And maybe after, the girlfriend will tell Sam to go to the little creek [to meet Jane]." Girlfriends, according to Marguerite and Kay, are people with whom girls can share their secrets and problems. Clandestine affairs, a boyfriend's rejection, the jealousy of a rival, and pregnancy are all topics that girls may only be able to talk about with their friends.

Some of the support that adolescent girls receive from the peer group is, no doubt, gained from observing and imitating the example of others. It is unlikely, for example, that the abiliy of several couples to marry despite prolonged parental opposition has gone unnoticed among the adolescents. Girls who are not yet involved with boys themselves may learn about the pleasures, and perils, of dating through observation or conversation with their peers.

ADOLESCENT STRATEGIES: CASE HISTORIES

To look at the specific means that adolescent girls employ to achieve their ends, this chapter returns to Kay, Marguerite, and Nora.

Marguerite and Nora employed similar strategies to counter adult maneuvers. Both girls refused to marry their promises and both repeatedly ran off with men of their choice. Nora and Marguerite also both got pregnant, Marguerite around June of 1981.

These two adolescents, like their mothers, said that it is necessary to have intercourse a number of times in order to conceive. Once is not enough (see also Berndt 1965b, 99; Meggitt 1962, 273; Cowlishaw 1979, 12; Hamilton 1981, 23).

To my knowledge, neither adolescent girls nor their partners used birth control devices. At the clinic, birth control devices were available to adolescents only if their parents requested them. In 1981 the clinic had received three indirect requests from parents that were never followed up, in two cases because the girls were discovered to be pregnant. I was able to speak to one man on the subject of birth control. He said that men did not do anything to prevent pregnancy in their partners. The extent to which young girls may have been employing indigenous birth control methods in 1981 is unknown. What is known of these methods indicates that they would not successfully prevent pregnancy. (For discussions of such methods see Cowlishaw 1979, 13–23 and Hamilton 1981, 20–21.)

Kay's discussion of several young girls who were pregnant in 1981, including Marguerite, suggests that as often as not, premarital pregnancy is an unintended and unwanted consequence of sexual activity:

> My girlfriend Vera wanted to marry [a young boy], but she can't. He's already married to a girl. . . . She made friend with an old boyfriend. . . . She's feeling embarrassed about having a child that she knows herself will be wrong side skin [that is, because the union was not straight there will be confusion about "what to call the child"]. And when it's born the families will be upset about it. . . . [Now for] Marguerite and Jenny. It's a bit different. They have different feelings. Marguerite is very happy and smiling. She likes to have the baby. But Jenny, she doesn't like to have the baby. But we say, "Too bad, she did it herself, she ended up pregnant." Sometimes when she has a pain she feels like crying and it's awful sad when her mother says, "Jenny's in pain." It makes me want to cry. Because she has the pain and she doesn't want the baby. Maybe when the baby is born she will like it a lot. . . . Marguerite likes to have the baby even though she is not married. . . . She will be a good mother. . . . But for a single girl who is pregnant, life is hard. Parents don't like single girls to be pregnant. They want them to be married before they get pregnant. Like when Claire had her baby, my mother [who is Claire's father's sister and guardian] was so cross that she wanted to kill [the baby]. . . . A single girl calls the name of the father of the baby and the father may say, "No, that's not my baby." That's how life starts for a single girl, a bit hard. The father refuses to be the father of the baby and it hurts

mother inside real bad. The girl didn't want to be pregnant when she was playing around with the man; that's what she'll think and say to herself.

Thus pregnancy may be as much an accident as an intended means of marrying a man of choice.

But pregnancy may also be capitalized on, if not actively sought. Nora's pregnancy undoubtedly was the deciding factor in her marriage, though whether or not she intended it for this end is unknown. Marguerite's pregnancy, however, may have been more of a conscious attempt to marry Brian: "Some girls have promised husbands. They don't like it when they do. They want to marry their boyfriend. They want to find [bear] a kid for their boyfriend so they can marry him."[13] Marguerite made this statement before she was pregnant. The following elaboration was made when she was at most a few days pregnant if she was pregnant at all: "Sometimes a family here don't like a girl in the first place. But when they get pregnant and they have that little baby and when they see that baby is true for their son, that baby has their son's face, they won't growl at that girl. They will feel ashamed [and let] them marry."

Marguerite perceives that pregnancy is a condition for which exceptions can be made; the fact that a couple is not straight may be overlooked if they have a child together. In the discussion in which this statement was made, Marguerite referred to another young girl and to the fact that she and her "wrong side" husband married after the birth of their child. This association suggests that the example of others, rather than her own condition, was the inspiration for this comment.

There have been a number of such examples to inspire young girls like Marguerite. Between 1978 and 1981, seven marriages of young girls were attributed to premarital pregnancy. Five of these unions were incorrect and all were marriages of choice.

But pregnancy did not lead to a marriage of choice for Marguerite, at least not in 1981.[14] Pregnancy alone is not a guarantee of marriage. This outcome still depends on parental consent and on male intent. Marguerite's continuing single status may have depended as much on the fact that Brian, like Tyler, found "another girl" as it did on Lily's continuing opposition to the match. A brief conversation that Marguerite and I had when she was about six months' pregnant suggests that the former may have been true in her case:

■ *I will stay single. When a girl is expecting those men are really nice to her only for money. I won't give any single boy money. When they ask I tell lies.*[15]

Did Lily tell you that?

I found out myself. When a girl is expecting they go find another girl. I'll stay single.

Between 1967 and 1981, fourteen other premarital pregnancies did not result in marriage to the child's reputed genitor.[16] In three of these cases young girls had not yet given birth when I left the field. Since more often than not marriage follows birth in such cases, marriage may have occured later. In another case the pregnancy miscarried. In another the mother and father of a child born in 1981 were attempting to marry but the girl's mother refused to allow the match. In the remaining nine cases all the children were living and at least three years of age in 1981, but the pregnancies had not resulted in marriage to the children's reputed genitors. Thus Marguerite and the other adolescent girls also have many examples of premarital pregnancies that have not led to a marriage of choice. This is a risk if indeed pregnancy is sought as a means of marrying a chosen partner. Like five of these women whose pregnancies did not lead to marriage with the children's fathers, Marguerite might marry another man at a later time. Or like two others she might continue to be a "single mother."[17]

Finally, let us look at Kay's case. Kay has, in a sense, chosen the partner chosen for her, insofar as she would "like to get married" to her promise. But what if Kay continues to respect her father's wishes that she remain unmarried.

"Unmarried woman" is not a concept that is labeled in the Aboriginal language of Mangrove. A *ngalanyjinyung* becomes a *maninyung* after marrying and bearing children. If she does not marry and bear children she remains a *ngalanyjinyung* until she becomes an "old woman." Even today, females who Westerners might regard as "single women" are lumped together, at least linguistically, with the young girls. This linguistic treatment of female status accords well with the ideal model of marriage; in it there is no place for an unmarried woman. Indeed, a female is, in a sense, born married if her mother has been bestowed as a mother-in-law. But here it is important to distinguish between "married" in the sense of betrothed and "married" in the de facto sense of actually living with a spouse (Shapiro 1979, 83). According to informants' recollections of pre-mission times, all mature women were not only married, they were de facto married, with the possible exception of the very old (see also Rose 1960, 79). There is no tradition for the status or role of spinster.

Spinsterhood, however, has been introduced to the people of Mangrove. The first spinsters were missionaries, women who came as nurses and teachers. Kay's mother's sister, Majiwi, was trained by one such woman, a nursing sister whose work at Mangrove extended from 1962 to 1980. In 1981 there were Aboriginal spinsters, of a sort, as well. When the mission began its campaign against polygyny, at least one married man with rights to other wives apparently renounced some of his rights, but not all of them. The man to whom Majiwi and her half sister were betrothed did not take Majiwi's half sister as his wife. But, according to mission records, he maintained that no one else could either.[18] It could be said that Majiwi's half sister is a married woman living apart from her husband. However, neither she nor Majiwi are regarded as married women; they are classified as young girls and presented as examples of single women. There were three other women beyond the age of twenty living at Mangrove who had never de facto married.[19] These women, who ranged in age from twenty-three to forty-seven in 1981, were all suffering from severe health problems at the time they might have married. The eldest, for example, had Hansen's disease.

Two of these five women had careers. Majiwi, of course, had her position as a health worker at the clinic. The other, an accredited teacher at the school, was Kay's neighbor and kinswoman. Should Kay remain a spinster, whether from choice or necessity, the precedent has been set by women who are of some, if not major, significance in her life.

There is one other recently introduced alternative to marriage with an assigned husband. In contemporary Mangrove, a young girl can step completely out of the system by marrying a white or by leaving the Aboriginal community for a "European" center such as Darwin (see also Gale 1970, 315).

Two young women from Mangrove had married whites. One was living with her husband in a town near Darwin; the other lived on another Aboriginal settlement. Marriage with whites is not, however, approved of in general. As Lily put it, "It leaves not enough people." Attempts, or perceived attempts, by whites to marry or date Aboriginal women at Mangrove have led to several incidents that include a broken nose, a stabbing, spear throwing, and litigation. A further risk of this alternative is suggested in the following statement of a mission woman: "a number of [adolescent girls] are not happy to marry Aboriginal men. They have seen some girls have good marriages with white men and they would like to do the same. They see the sort of marriage [Dolores] has with [Morton]. But they probably won't find this. They are more likely to get the dregs like [Meredith and Donna]."

The latter two women referred to here, Donna and Meredith, were both in Darwin in 1981, having first gone there in 1976 and 1977 respectively. Both had successfully staved off others' attempts to place them with Aboriginal husbands they did not want. Donna, who is Lily's younger sister, refused to marry the man her mother had bestowed her upon, even resisting an attempt, in which her mother colluded, to take her by force. Meredith had escaped from marriage with a man who had attempted to take her as a second wife. Both young women had lived with white men but neither was married, even de facto, by 1981.

But "town" without marriage, an alternative taken by several women from Mangrove, is perceived, by at least some, to be even worse. According to Lily, it is a place for the "lost," a place for drinking "grog" and being "mad for man." As Marguerite said of one young woman who had returned to Mangrove and presumably told tales of her adventures in town, "When Martha is in Darwin she gets married to lots of white fellas, this one and the next one, and the next one."

In September of 1981, I went to Darwin to return a vehicle before the wet closed down the roads in and out of Mangrove. One day shortly after noon, as I stood looking over some cassettes in the local Woolworth's, I was greeted by one of Mangrove's seventeen-year-old girls. With spirit-scented breath she asked me if I were going back to Mangrove. "Yes," I replied, "are you?" "No, I'm staying her for . . . ," then gave the hand sign for "grog." As she was leaving she said, in what can only be described as an ironic tone, "Give my husband my love." Then she laughed and turned and walked away.

DISCUSSION

The adolescent expectations about men and marriage described in this chapter have been presented largely in terms of statements made by Marguerite, Nora, and Kay. Members of the opposite sex are important to each of the three young girls; their actions have the potential for making the girls feel good or bad. All three girls want, at least in the best of all possible worlds, to get married. Nora and Marguerite want to have children; Kay and Nora want to perform the adult female role. All, however, expressed concerns about the character or behavior of men they might marry. For Kay and Nora there seem to be good men and bad men, or better perhaps, men who are well behaved or not. For Marguerite, all the men that she might marry are not to be relied on. The qualities of greatest importance are fidelity and control of jealous and aggressive impulses. Both Marguerite and Kay indicated that whether or not a man is straight or bestowed is a factor to be considered when choosing a partner. But only Kay seemed willing to actually consider such factors when making decisions about her own life. It can only be assumed that the expectations of Kay, Marguerite, and Nora represent those of other adolescent girls at Mangrove. But insofar as the young girls of this small, closely knit community have experiences similar to those of these three young girls, it seems a safe and reasonable assumption.

The concerns of the three girls are not, for the most part, considerations for members of the adult generations, at least when they are arranging a girl's marriage or considering whether or not they should consent to her union. Of major significance to parents is whether or not partners are straight, bestowed, or square back for a previous marriage.

This then is the substance of the battle over marriage: adults want to arrange their children's marriages, adolescents want to choose for themselves, and the criteria for mate selection are different for each generation.

The extent to which Aboriginal girls have always resisted being married to husbands not of their choosing cannot be known. However, the newly created period of maidenhood at Mangrove, in juxtaposition with institutions that present choice of marriage partner as a legitimate marriage strategy and provide an environment in which such a strategy may be pursued, has likely encouraged resistance. Some of the means of resistance are clearly products of the new sociocultural environment; neither premarital pregnancy nor remaining single were viable strategies in the days when all girls, at least ideally, married before they were fecund. Nor, of course, could Aboriginal maidens escape to European centers before the coming of the Europeans.

■ 5
Conclusion

At least in theory, the Aboriginal people of Mangrove once channeled and controlled the sexuality of their adolescent females. They arranged the marriages of their female children before they were born and placed them with their husbands before menarche. Thus, adolescent girls were married women. By the time they achieved reproductive capabilities, their sexual impulses had been directed toward men deemed appropriate husbands by their society. Young wives might have extramarital affairs—female sexuality could not be completely controlled by early marriage—but adultery is another kind of problem with different potential solutions.

In contemporary Mangrove, the solution of premenarcheal marriage is no longer an available alternative. Such a marriage practice was not in accord with the Australian commonwealth's laws. The missionaries imposed the legal marriage age of sixteen on the settlement's dwellers in an attempt to eradicate early marriage. Their success is indicated by today's average female marriage age of seventeen, more than three years after the average age of menarche. Maidenhood, a period of time between menarche and marriage, has thus become a part of the female adolescent experience for the Aborigines of Mangrove.

According to Aboriginal theory, the premenarcheal marriage age fit well with the system of arranged marriage. Girls could be placed with their husbands while they were still young, before romantic inclinations and the resolve to have one's own way could develop. While a period of maidenhood does not necessarily preclude arranged marriage, the missionaries discouraged this Aboriginal practice as well. The conjunction of relatively mature unmarried females and an ideal based on Western marriage practices resulted in the radical modification of the indigenous marriage system.

Many aspects of settlement life either give legitimacy to the idea of choosing a marriage partner or provide the means of doing so. Romantic love, for example, is a constant theme in the Hollywood movies and popular music that adolescents are exposed to throughout much of their lives. Similarly, there are many opportunities to interact with members of the opposite sex at the school, a place where adolescents spend the majority of their days.

Acceptance of the largely imposed changes in marriage is not, however, universal and appears to vary with age or position in the system. Adults, who are still held responsible for the marriages of their children, have not generally accepted the idea that adolescents should choose for themselves. While for many adolescents, marriage to a partner not of their own choosing is unacceptable. The period of maidenhood today is the time when parents attempt to see that their daughters are married correctly and the time when adolescent girls resist their parents' efforts. Thus female adolescence at Mangrove is a life stage characterized by intergenerational conflict over marriage.

Adolescent sexuality need not be regulated by early marriage. Alternatively, societies may institute various norms governing premarital sex and impose various sanctions against those who break the rules. At present, the adults of Mangrove seem to be taking this tack as a means of channeling adolescent female sexuality. However, their concern is less with sexuality per se than with the choice of marriage partners.

Contrasting adult response to the sexual behavior of adolescent girls at Mangrove and at Holman—a community of settled Copper Inuit in the Canadian Arctic studied by Richard Condon as a part of the Harvard Adolescence Project—is informative.[1] Employing a framework for the study of adolescence similar to that used at Mangrove, he has noted similarites in the precontact levels of social complexity of these former nomadic foragers and in their recent experiences of rapid and extreme social change (Condon 1987, 194). He has also noted similarites in the former marriage arrangements of these two groups of people (pp. 194–195). Before settling, Copper Inuit girls commonly joined their husbands before or at menarche in marriages arranged by their parents (p. 56). At the time of Condon's fieldwork, however, in the early 1980s, Inuit girls were marrying later; they were also, for the most part, choosing their own partners, engaging in premarital sex, and in some cases getting pregnant before they got married (pp. 144, 150, 154–155).

While the behavior of these adolescents appears to parallel much of that displayed by the young girls of Mangrove, adult reactions to adolescent sexual behavior in the two communities are strikingly different. In the Inuit community of Holman today, adolescent sexuality is "unaccompanied by any serious parental surveillance or disapproval" and parents are "tolerant and accepting" of the premarital pregnancies of their daughters (Condon 1987, 143, 150).

Condon suggests that prior to settlement, when the sparse population was scattered and male mortality high, early betrothal was motivated by an Inuit "concern that offspring obtain any reasonable partner" (Condon 1987, 56, 195). He also notes that even when Inuit parents arranged the marriages of their children, a girl "could refuse to marry her betrothed" (p. 56). Furthermore adolescent couples might change their minds, and change partners before settling down (pp. 57, 141, 195). The acquiescence of girls to the plans of others appears to have always been less critical for the Copper Inuit than for the Australian Aborigines. If Condon's surmise is correct, today, in the security of the settlement where an increasing population of adolescent boys and girls has the opportunity to interact day in and day out, it is not surprising to find that early betrothal appears be an arrangement that is no longer regarded as necessary by older Inuit people (pp. 155, 195). At Holman, parents have little control over their children's selection of a spouse, and it is generally accepted that "the ultimate decision rests with the child" (pp. 57, 155).

It is unclear whether the premenarcheal marriage age of Inuit girls was ever perceived as a means of controlling their sexual behavior or whether premarital sexuality was ever a matter of concern in Inuit society. Premenarcheal marriage need not always be a means of controlling adolescent sexuality. A cross-cultural study undertaken as a part of the Harvard Adolescence Project noted, for example, that early marriage for females was characteristic of the majority of societies surveyed (Whiting, Burbank, and Ratner 1986, 289). John Whiting has pointed out that such an arrangement "makes use of the full female reproductive span" and has suggested that early marriage among foragers allows women "to start having children as soon as possible to compensate for a low birth rate" (pp. 288, 290). At Holman today, parents are concerned that girls who bear children be sufficiently mature to care for them. Thus, pregnancy rather than sexual intercourse may be discouraged (Condon 1987, 143). The sexual behavior of Inuit maidens can thus be seen as an issue apart from that of marriage—one to be condemned or condoned by Inuit society on the basis of other criteria.

At Mangrove, however, girls' sexual behavior is perceived by adults as a threat to the system insofar as it may lead through pregnancy or habituation to an incorrect marriage. Enforced chastity may be the incidental outcome of parental attempts to see that their daughters do not marry incorrect partners. Nevertheless, parents are attempting to replace the controls of early marriage with a period of sexual abstinence for sexually mature females. The fights announcing adolescent affairs and what appears to be a growing rate of premarital pregnancy suggest that these efforts are not yet successful and that a new system of regulation has yet to take hold. This is far from surprising as there is little evidence for a tradition of teaching against premarital sexual behavior. Given the premenarcheal marriage age of past times, such teaching would have been superfluous.

For the adolescent girls of Mangrove, on the other hand, maidenhood is a time for choosing a husband. Their sexuality may be one means of doing so, or at least of doing so when faced with parental opposition. In particular, premarital pregnancy may be perceived by adolescent girls as a means of marrying a partner of choice.

Some of the adolescent girls who are choosing their own husbands are making bad choices, not only from the adult perspective but also in terms of their own criteria. Nora, for example, chose a man who abandoned her and her infant daughter after little more than a year of marriage. Other examples of poor marriage choices might be young men who do nothing but gamble, are excessively jealous and aggressive, or are chronically in jail. According to adults, negative qualities such as these are more likely to be found among young men, the men that adolescent girls prefer. However, making a bad choice may be less critical than it would be in other times or other circumstances. Nora is no longer married, but she is not trying to raise her daughter alone. The Australian government provides some financial support with Supporting Parents Benefit, and her family, particularly her mother Rosalind, is always there to guide and assist her.

Alternatively, maidenhood may be a period when adolescent girls attempt to remain unmarried. Urbanized Westerners are accustomed to situations of relative anonymity where individual behavior appears to have little immediate effect on social norms and practices. In a small community like Mangrove, however, there is little anonymity, and the intimate details of what we regard as "private life" are often common knowledge. In such circumstances, the impact that just one individual's behavior may have on others' expectations can be considerable. A number of young girls, for example, were aware of Nora's unhappy marital history and seemed to take some warning from it. And Nora is not the only girl to have suffered from male perfidy. The number of schoolgirls who chose to "stay single" as well as the positions on marriage taken by Kay and Marguerite suggest that marriage, whether arranged or voluntary, is beginning to be perceived by adolescent girls as something to be postponed, perhaps indefinitely.

But where would single status leave the young girls of Mangrove? On the settlement today, there is basically one adult female role, that entailed by marriage. An adult female, a woman, is a wife and a mother. She cooks for her husband and cares for her children. Women may also have jobs, in the Western sense of the word, but these occupations do not define, or contribute to, their status as adults. Indeed, jobs are far from plentiful, and as likely as not, work may be just a passing experience for the Aboriginal women of the settlement. It is generally expected that adult female life is spent as someone's wife and someone's mother.

The precedent for spinsterhood has been established, however, and it may be that more young girls will choose to remain single in the future. If a greater number do, their reproductive possibilities become a major question. Will unmarried women also be childless women or will they be single mothers? A related question is Will many more men act like Tyler and abandon their wives and children to the care of others? Assuming that neither Nora nor Marguerite marry, there is likely to be little difference between their family circumstances and that of their daughters, though in our scheme of things Nora is a "divorcee" and Marguerite an "unwed mother."

The experiences and behavior of adolescent girls may not affect simply the expectations of their peers. They may also be altering some of the basic principles of social organization and on-the-ground social structures of their community.

Concern with what to "call the child" of an incorrect union suggests that from the Aboriginal perspective, children of incorrect unions have the potential to disrupt the system of kin classification. The importance of maintaining a degree of coherence between marriage and kin classification is seen in the following example where marriage itself led to an alteration in terms: Rosalind once called a man "mother's father" when he was married to her "close" "mother's mother." When he left her and subsequently married a woman who was one of Rosalind's "close" "sisters," Rosalind called him "husband." Similar examples from Aboriginal communities across Australia indicate that this is not an issue of Aboriginal social organization confined to Mangrove (see for example, Kaberry 1939, 117–124; Piddington 1970; Turner 1974, 58, 203; Tonkinson 1978, 49). As Kaberry has noted (1939, 122), there is a certain amount of resilience in the system that can compensate for an incorrect union.[2] This resilience, however, undoubtedly has limits. There is a point beyond which the reassignment of kin terms to take into account incorrect unions and the children of those unions could render the system meaningless for those who use it. What this point might be and when and if it will be reached remain to be seen.

The development of a family and household organization

that parallels that described for Afro-Americans (see Stack 1974, for example) may be another such change. With single mothers like Nora residing with their parents and depending upon their financial and social resources, such a social arrangement may already be developing in the community (see also Koepping 1977, 171; Eckermann 1977, 298–299).

Perhaps the most important changes that are being ushered in by adolescent behavior are changes in gender relations, particularly those between husband and wife. It is my impression, after having spent more than two years in the company of couples like Marguerite's mother and father, that emotional intimacy and economic interdependence characterize the relationships of adult married couples at Mangrove. Lily, for example, often spoke, with what seemed like some pride, of Goodman's hunting ability and his provisioning of the family with fish. In turn, women like Lily appeared to take their role as housewives seriously, ensuring that at least damper and tea were prepared afresh for each of the three daily meals. Such couples were frequently seen in each other's company; affection was expressed between them through gestures (such as a pat) and tone of voice. While these impressions are far from adequate for establishing the extent and kind of changes that may be taking place, they do suggest that the relationships that girls like Marguerite and Nora are establishing with the fathers of their children are far different. However, I am comparing the relationships of adolescents with couples who have been married for twenty or thirty years. It may be that thirty years from now, the relationship between Tyler and Nora will be described by some future observer as one of cooperation and friendship.

The relationships of adolescent girls and their partners at Mangrove today should also be compared to those of spouses in pre-mission times. Again, because of lack of information about Aboriginal life during this period, this discussion must rely on the accounts of other ethnographers and the statements of informants who once lived as nomads. According to Rose, Aboriginal men were once the center of family life; women clustered around them creating "collectives of co-wives," groups that could be relied on for assistance during the childbearing and child rearing years. Husbands were older men at the peak of their productivity who supplied their wives with meat while receiving the women's vegetable products in turn (Rose 1968, 201, 206–208). If one accepts this model of pre-mission family life, Nora and, probably, Marguerite are living in very different circumstances vis-á-vis the fathers of their children.

Other descriptions of nomadic Aborigines suggest, however, that Rose's characterization may not capture the past reality of many Aboriginal households. For example, there is widespread agreement that Aboriginal women were once the primary food producers (Bell 1983, 54–55; Berndt 1965b, 97; Cowlishaw 1979, 220; Hamilton 1975, 171; Hiatt 1974, 10, 12; Warner 1969, 129; but cf. Altman 1984). It has been estimated that their gathered product accounted for between 50 percent to 80 percent in some desert areas (Hiatt 1974, 12) and between 60 percent to 90 percent in Arnhem Land (Peterson 1974, 22); these contributions may well have included significant amounts of protein as well as vegetable foodstuffs (Hamilton 1980–1981, 11). When women supplied food during times of ceremonial activity, male economic dependence on women was nearly complete (Warner 1969, 129; Peterson 1974, 22; Hamilton, 1980–1981, 15). What may be more critical for evaluating the connubial relations of nomadic times is Hamilton's observation that ordinarily the spheres of production and consumption were so gender-specific that there might be little exchange between husband and wife (Hamilton 1980–1981, 12–13).

This previous reliance on Aboriginal women's economic contribution is important, especially in light of the possible development of a "consanguineal household" (Gonzales 1970, 232; 1984). Male unemployment and reduction of male power are factors that are frequently associated with such a household in other parts of the world (Gonzales 1970, 241–242; 1984, 8–9; Whitehead 1978, 818). Aboriginal men have undoubtedly been peripheralized to some extent by the advent of Western institutions, particularly those relating to law and authority, and now are largely unemployed in terms of Western jobs. But it is women's economic contribution that has become "redundant" with the introduction of a cash economy (Hamilton 1975, 173). Young girls like Kay who live off their own earnings and young girls like Nora and Marguerite who provide for themselves and their children with their Supporting Parents Benefit might see little difference between themselves and women who once supported themselves and their children largely by their own hunting and gathering efforts.

Several aspects of the prior system of marriage and household organization also raise questions about the possibilities for conjugal intimacy in previous times. Cowlishaw has observed, for example, that when there is a great disparity of age between spouses, as there often was when premanarcheal marriage age was the norm, husbands and wives spend little time together and have few activities in common (Cowlishaw 1979, 217–218). Polygyny may also have worked against the development of connubial intimacy. For example, the Whitings have suggested that cosleeping can serve as an indicator of husband/wife intimacy (Whiting and Whiting 1975, 199). Yet the sleeping arrangements of a polygynous household at best included a husband sleeping by the side of each wife in turn and at worst a husband ignoring all but one wife or sleeping apart from all of his wives.

In the past, a husband was probably years older, often absent, and when present likely to be interested in another wife. In contrast, co-wives spent their days together as they gathered, prepared food, and cared for their children. These women were often clan "sisters" if not actual biological sisters whose shared backgrounds may have facilitated their cooperation and friendship (Murdock 1949, 30–31). Under these circumstances, Aboriginal women may well have formed stronger bonds with their co-wives than with their husbands. (Cowlishaw 1979, 200–202; Berndt 1965b, 94–95). Aboriginal women of the past may also have had their mothers as intimates. A man would often reside near his wife's parents, particularly when his wife was young (Peterson 1974, 23; Shapiro 1973). In addition, women as mothers-in-law were quite ready to live near their sons-in-law to ensure that their gifts continued (Shapiro 1979, 24). Again the circumstances of Marguerite, Kay, and Nora, insofar as the shared intimacy of their domestic interaction is with mothers and sisters rather than husbands, may bear more resemblance to the past than is first apparent.

Nevertheless, the Aborigines of Mangrove in 1981 were living a life that bore little resemblance to that of their ancestors. For at least twenty-nine years, since the establishment of the mission in 1952, a myriad of institutions, individuals, and edicts had impinged upon the Aboriginal world, transforming aspects of their life beyond recognition. The missionaries perceived that their efforts to change the Aboriginal people of Mangrove would be best served by concentrating on the young.[3] It is thus not surprising that many of the efforts to change Aboriginal society can be seen in the adolescents. In this sense the adolescent girls of Mangrove are vehicles of social change. At the moment it appears that their behavior may deal the final blow to at least one aspect of the society: the marriage system. This, however, depends on the extent to which they do or do not return, as many of their mothers have, to acting in terms of indigenous principles. The question is In another generation will their present behavior, seen today by adults as lawless, come to be seen as a manifestation of the Law?

■ Appendix

I am going to read you a story and then we will talk about it:

> When Jane was a little girl her mother promised her to Bert. All the time that Jane has been growing up, Bert has been giving Jane and her mother dugong, fish, money, clothes, and other nice things. Now Jane is big and her mother is saying she should marry Bert. But at school Jane met Sam. She likes him very much and he is straight for her. She would like to marry Sam.

1. If you were Jane what would you do? Why?
2. If you were Jane's mother what would you do? Why?
3. If you were Bert what would you do? Why?
4. If you were Sam what would you do? Why?
5. If you were Jane and didn't know what to do, would you talk to somebody? Who? What do you think they would do?
6. Why do you think Jane wants to marry Sam not Bert?
7. Why do you think Jane's mother wants her to marry Bert? Why now?
8. Do you think some mothers here think like Jane's mother? Do you think your mother thinks like Jane's mother?
   (These two questions were dropped after a couple of interviews were administered. They appeared to make informants uncomfortable and yielded little information.)
9. What do you think Jane's uncle would do?
10. What do you think Jane's father would do?
11. If girls aren't promised, how do they get a husband these days?

■ Notes

1. Mangrove is a pseudonym as are all personal names used in this work.

2. This is at approximately Stage Two on Tanner's Ratings (see Buckler 1979, 44–45).

3. Full fecundity does not necessarily coincide with menarche (Tanner 1978, 66). There may follow a period of several months or years of subfecundity referred to by some as "adolescent sterility" (Montagu 1979).

4. Information on whether adolescent girls had begun to menstruate was collected on twelve adolescent girls ranging in age from twelve to nineteen. Sources of this information include the girls themselves, their mothers or guardians, and the settlement nurse to whom girls had reported. In six cases it was possible to determine the age (in years) at menarche. The average for these six cases is 13.7, the median 13.5. Note the close correspondence between these figures and Rose's estimate that girls on Groote Eylandt begin menstruating between the ages of thirteen and fourteen (Rose 1960, 65, 67). Reliable data on the average age of menarche in other Australian Aboriginal populations are all but nonexistent. It is beyond the scope of this study to attempt to ascertain if there has been a decrease in the age of menarche as there has been in other world areas (Eveleth and Tanner 1975). Given changes in such factors as diet, amount of exercise, and the use of Western medicine, it is possible that the average age of menarche is earlier today than in previous times (Zacharias and Wurtman 1969; Frisch et al. 1981).

5. Annette Hamilton has outlined a similar problem for the Aboriginal people of Maningrida (1975, 176; 1981, 17–18).

6. As Broude (1975) has pointed out, the reasons people give for

discouraging or prohibiting premarital sexual behavior vary from society to society. For example, the Riffans and Kazak "prohibit premarital intercourse to insure the virginity of their girls before marriage," whereas the Wogeo, Goajiro, and Javanese discourage premarital sex because it is "equated with postmarital promiscuity" (Broude 1975, 382–383). If the focus of inquiry is limited to the cultural perception of social problems, it might be more appropriate to say that the Kazak are concerned with virginity, the Javanese with postmarital promiscuity, and the Aborigines of Mangrove with marriage. On the other hand, to ignore the common element of each of these concerns, the possibility of premarital sexual behavior, is to ignore one of the "givens" of human life that may provide a framework for cross-cultural comparison (Kluckhohn 1953, 521, in Goodenough 1970, 2).

7. Clearly, the problems posed by human sexuality are not limited to premarital intercourse. Extramarital sex, for example, may also be perceived by the social group as a behavior to be regulated or prohibited. As parents and guardians of adolescents, however, the adults of Mangrove were primarily concerned about the behavior of the unmarried. Thus this discussion is confined to the topic of premarital sexuality.

CHAPTER 2: THE RESEARCH SETTING

1. People speaking one Aboriginal language have predominated at Mangrove since its establishment. They accounted for a majority of its population in 1981. In this work, discussions of past social forms are confined to those of this group. However, in 1977–1978 and in 1981 the settlement was home to people who spoke, or once spoke, at least five or six other Australian languages. In spite of their diverse histories, the Aborigines of Mangrove formed a tightly localized, interacting populations. Social intercourse was by no means confined to members of a kindred, country group, clan, or language group. All members of the population were able to converse in the language of the predominant group or in Kriol. People from other linguistic backgrounds did not form obviously separate subgroups. All were integrated into the larger community through ties of kinship and marriage. Many shared the experience of living at Mangrove for decades and appeared to share the concerns of the majority for the problems of the young. I believe it is appropriate to regard the people of Mangrove as a unit to be associated with a "public culture" (Goodenough 1971; Whiting 1968).

2. Between 1903 and 1908 the Eastern and African Cold Storage Company kept between five thousand and six thousand cattle near the northern boundary of the area once occupied by the majority of Aborigines at Mangrove (Bauer 1964, 157). During these years local Aborigi-

nes were systematically exterminated by the cattle company (Merlan 1978, 86; Bauer 1964, 157). Cole claims that "a number of the ancestors of those living at [Mangrove] today were killed in this way" (Cole 1982, 14). The evidence he presents in support of this statement, however, is only inferential. Thompson, who traveled in the Mangrove area in 1935, reported that he found the people, who were then nomadic hunters and gatherers, "well fed and in good condition." Children were also "numerous" (Thompson 1935–1936, 8–9). He also reported, however, that in the Arnhem Land Reserve "the native population has greatly decreased" (p. 42).

3. This number is based on my census figure of 420 inhabitants of Mangrove as of March 1981. Year-round residents of the outstations (discussed later in this chapter) are not included in this census. They might total another 50 or 60 people.

4. Many of the village houses were old and falling apart, and sometimes the house of a dead person would be torn down or leveled with a bulldozer. Bayarra's house, however, had been built only three or four years before her husband's death. It was in relatively good condition and so was left standing to be reoccupied when thought properly cleansed. Two of the five houses standing vacant during my 1981 residence survey were left so for this reason.

5. A sample of fifteen monthly reports on employment sent by the mission to the welfare office of the Northern Territory between 1958 and 1974 suggests that the low rate of employment is due, at least in part, to a limited number of jobs on the settlement, in spite of increases in population. For example, in July of 1958 when the potential male work force numbered 41, 35 males were employed. In that year when the potential female work force was 53, 38 were employed. In January of 1973, however, when the potential work force of males and females was 77 and 67 respectively, only 40 males and 19 females were employed. Numbers of Aborigines listed in these reports as "self-employed" or employed in "handicraft" manufacture and "home duties" suggests that there may have been fewer job openings than people who wanted to work (based on Monthly Welfare Letters, July 1958–January 1974).

6. This age range is that used in the settlement's welfare reports. I have computed these percentages using the Department of Aboriginal Affairs census for 1981 (which gives the population of Mangrove as 490) because it also makes this age division.

7. This description is largely based on interviews and on sixty-two spot observations of Kay, forty-two of Nora, and fifty-five of Marguerite. It is also based on numerous spot observations of other adolescent girls and boys. These observations, made over the nine-month period of fieldwork, recorded each adolescent's location, companions, and activi-

ties. Most of the observations were made during the day. They do not include observations of adolescents in my house.

8. The intoxication that results from petrol inhalation has been described as "disinhibiting" and hallucinatory (Brady and Morice 1982, 73, 82–83). According to Marguerite and one of her girlfriends, petrol sniffing "makes you mad; screaming and laughing." The origin of this practice, which today is widespread among the youth of many Aboriginal communities, is variously ascribed to Australian (Money et al. 1970, 395) or American (Brady and Morice 1982, 72) servicemen stationed in the Northern Territory during World War II. Petrol may be the only means of intoxication in a community where alcohol is banned and drugs all but unknown (Money et al. 1970, 395). Though even repeated sniffing does not necessarily produce any obvious long-term health effects (MacAndrew and Edgerton in Brady and Morice 1982, 73), petrol sniffing may be accompanied by the "detrimental and irreversible effects of lead [accumulation]," severe burns, and death (Brady and Morice 1982, 73). At Mangrove, petrol sniffers were, for the most part, adolescent boys and girls. I was told of fifteen males and ten females who were said to sniff petrol in 1981. Petrol sniffing and the acts of theft and vandalism performed by petrol sniffers were decried by many Aboriginal adults and resident whites. The explanations for petrol sniffing offered by outside observers are many, ranging from parental neglect and poor home environment to an act of defiance (Brady and Morice 1982). Similarly, many explanations for petrol sniffing are offered by the Aboriginal adults and adolescents of Mangrove. These include the temptation or bad influence of others, boredom, lack of parental control, a reaction to parental anger precipitated by other adolescent behaviors, and, for male sniffers, a means of "making trouble for girls," that is, a means of protesting their lack of a girlfriend or wife.

9. In many cases, when a woman is pregnant, at least one of her husband's brothers, sisters, or other kin dreams of the child to be born. They inform the parents of their dream and subsequently stand in a special relationship to the child. According to my informants, children are transferred from their countries to their mothers by means of such dreams. (For some examples of conception dreams see Goodale 1971, 141–142 and Warner 1937, 21–22.) However, a child may be dreamt from a country other than that of its father (see also Shapiro 1979, 17; Merlan n.d.). In this case, the child is said to come from the country that is specified in the dream but shares his father's clan and moiety. Also note that clans and moieties are not groups that undertake collective actions, but social categories that order social relations (see also Shapiro 1979, 33).

10. This figure is based on the age of first marriage for sixty-six males living at Mangrove in 1981.

11. There were also approximately eight bachelors over the age of thirty at Mangrove during the period of study. I do not include these in the discussion here for two reasons. First, I observed them and their activities even less frequently than I observed the younger set of young boys. Second, none of them ever came to my attention as perpetrators of the behaviors (discussed later in this chapter) that seemed characteristic of the younger people. This suggests an obvious but important point: maturational age, not just the social position of adolescent males, is a factor that must be taken into account in explanations of adolescent behavior.

12. Tindale estimates that this occurred between the ages of ten and thirteen (Tindale 1925–1926, 68). Rose estimates that circumcision on Groote Eylandt took place at about age nine (Rose 1960, 20).

13. The women of Mangrove have other roles in the indigenous religion. They either have their own separate versions of a ceremony or take part with the men at certain points in the ritual celebrations. In ceremonies that took place in 1978 and 1981, older female participants remarked on the absence of younger ones. When I asked why younger women did not take part, I was told they were "shy," not interested, or too busy playing cards. I was also told that before the imposition of white law, girls who refused to participate would have been speared. It is not likely that Christian conversion alone can account for the absence of young women from these ceremonies. Few of them were Christians and many baptized Christians still participated in the ceremonies (see also Berndt 1950, 61–62).

14. When Marguerite was five or six, one of Lily's classifactory but "close" "father's sisters" had asked for Marguerite and her younger sister to raise as her own. This is a customary request from childless women, and Lily, who had four other children besides the two girls, agreed to it. Marguerite's younger sister did not wish to leave her mother, however, so only Marguerite went to live with her "mother's father's sister" and her husband.

15. In 1978 when many parents did take school-age children to the outstations during the school year, there was talk of fines for absenteeism and withholding of "child checks," a government allowance paid to the parents of schoolchidren. Though I do not know if such financial penalties were ever actually imposed, the threat in itself may have contributed to the smaller outstation populations in 1981.

CHAPTER 3: MARRIAGE PAST AND PRESENT
1. Throughout this work I present statements made by the people of Mangrove. These are derived from my notes of interviews and conversations. In these notes I attempted to record statements verbatim.

However, I have translated some of these into American English to make them intelligible (see Colby 1966). For readability I have also cleaned up some of these statements. For example, I have deleted false starts and duplication.

2. *Gajali* is the self-reciprocal term for mother-in-law/son-in-law. *Gagu* is the self-reciprocal term for MM:MMB/DC.

3. From the perspective of a male ego, the ideal form of marriage is with a classificatory "MMBDD" whose mother comes from the country of his actual mother's mother and mother's mother's brother.

4. According to Turner, the paternal role in marriage arrangements on Groote Eylandt is an innovation encouraged by the missionaries (1974, 62ff.). But see Shapiro (1981, 64–66), who argues against such an interpretation, and Hiatt (1967, 473–474).

5. *Laga* refers to the calf of the leg. In sign language this part of the body symbolizes "brother" or "sister." *Ngura* means "fire" or "firewood" and is used as a synonym for "wife."

6. Seclusion at menarche, ritual defloration, introcision, and ritual plural intercourse are elements that are often associated with female puberty ceremonies in Aborginal Australia (Cowlishaw 1979, 125–130). According to Berndt, in pre-mission times, ritual defloration of young girls was included in a ceremony held by people in the Mangrove area (Berndt 1951a, 67, 68). One older woman, familiar with the ritual defloration practices of people living to the south of Mangrove, said that such ceremonies did not take place at Mangrove. The four other women with whom I talked about ceremonies at menarche talked only about seclusion. In the past, girls were secluded in their "mother's mother's" camp, where they observed certain dietary and behavioral restrictions until the flow ceased (see also Hamilton 1981, 19–20; Reid 1983, 79). Another woman claimed that currently a brief ceremony is performed for girls when they first begin to menstruate. I was unable to confirm this statement with any other informant, and six women said there was no ceremony of any kind today. One woman who answered in the negative said that such a ceremony would "embarrass a girl here." Indeed, in 1981 menarche often seemed to be kept a secret. Only two of the mothers or guardians interviewed about adolescent girls said that their daughters had told them when they began to menstruate. Several informants said that girls tell no one. It is possible that girls do not want their parents or other adults to know that they have begun menstruating because of the association between intercourse and menarche. For example: "Last year Elaine got her period because she was going with some man. If a girl goes with men she gets her period. Some take a long time before they get it, but some get it quick if they go everyday with a boy." (Burbank in press; see also Goodale 1971, 45; Hamilton 1981, 19; Warner 1937, 64, 481).

7. Apparently, Warner's informants gave a similar explanation for premenarcheal marriage; he states, "A young girl often starts living in her husband's household before menstruation. The 'dué' [husband] usually takes her for fear of having her stolen from her parents by some other dué" (Warner 1937:65).

8. He was also expected to contribute to his mother-in-law's brothers, mothers, father, and her husband. This obligation continued for as long as these people lived.

9. To reciprocate for their sons-in-law's gifts, the women of Mangrove provide their sons-in-law with tea, damper, and other cooked food.

10. Co-wives who do not call each other sister may call each other *gagu*, that is "MM/DD."

11. Rose observed three older women, between the ages of fifty-eight and sixty-eight, living apart from their husbands (Rose 1960, 79). He also quotes Webb's observation that men "discard and almost entirely neglect their aged wives, who are then usually cared for in the camps of married daughters" (Webb 1944, 28–29, quoted in Rose 1960, 79).

12. I have defined "adult" female as one born before 1961. I have chosen this year because nearly all the females described as "young girls," that is, not yet adult, were born after it.

13. These are defined as marriages where both spouses were living and regarded as married by December of 1981. I have not, for example, included the marriage of Nora and Tyler because they were separated and regarded as no longer married by the end of the year. Tyler's new marriage to Claire is included, however.

14. This sample is reasonably representative of the age distribution of married women. The first number given after the years represents the total number of women in effective unions by the end of 1981 in that age-group; the second number represents the number of histories obtained from that age-group: 1900–1920: 3/3; 1921–1930: 7/3; 1931–1940: 7/6; 1941–1950: 19/8; 1951–1960: 28/16; 1961–1970: 15/12.

15. At Mangrove it is said that the genitor of a child gives it his face and feet. (Feet mark the individuality of a person much like a face; the footprints that each person leaves are recognized as distinctive.) Similarly, a child born with hair on its arms is said to be the child of its mother's husband.

CHAPTER 4: CONTEMPORARY MARRIAGE

1. Working on Margaret K. Bacon's study of parental perception of children's behavior (Rutgers University, 1974–1980). I became

acquainted with the use of dilemmas for this purpose. While this technique might resemble that used in cross-cultural studies of moral development, this was not my intent. For the list of questions that followed that dilemma, see the appendix.

2. Alcoholic beverages became accessible to the people of Mangrove as never before with the establishment of a nearby mining town in 1966. All the women with whom I spoke about alcohol associated drinking with drunkenness and aggressive behavior. Mangrove has maintained its status as a "dry" community, most recently through the efforts of its female population.

3. The fact that these answers contain relatively few reasons for the choices is likely due to the written mode of response. Although this was preferable to verbal communication—I have mentioned that many girls simply would not talk to me—it is not a medium in which adolescents had, by and large, a great deal of fluency.

4. By the end of the study Andy and Ella were again living together. It was unclear if Violet and her husband would stay married.

5. This was a slightly revised version of Kohlberg's Heinz Dilemma (Kohlberg 1981).

6. A question about this category of boys was suggested by John and Beatrice Whiting. While I found no exact counterpart at Mangrove, the words "show off" were occasionally used in Aboriginal English and the question was relevant enough to elicit some interesting answers, as Marguerite's reply shows. Note that her reply also indicates that the meaning given to "show off" at Mangrove is not quite the meaning it has in American English.

7. "Bludging," I was told by a white Australian, once meant living off the earnings of a prostitute. Today in both Australian and Aboriginal English it refers to people who take without giving back in return. Boys and girls who bludge at Mangrove are those who live at home after school without contributing to the family's income. Neither Brian nor Ginny were employed during the study period.

8. This phrase probably refers to the fact that this boy and girl had been engaging in sexual intercourse over a period of time, long enough for impregnation to have occurred according to Aboriginal theory. It probably does not refer to an actual pregnancy.

9. Marguerite replied to the question as follows: "No. He shouldn't have to steal the medicine and think about breaking into the man's shop if he didn't like his wife, but if he thought of stealing the medicine out of the man's shop that means he likes his wife to be alive and not dead." Kay said: "If he didn't love his wife very much he wouldn't steal the medicine. But if he did love her he would still go ahead and steal it. . . . [He wouldn't steal it if he didn't love his wife because] his love for the woman, his wife, it floated away, it's no more." Note that each of the

three gave answers that were interpretations of Billy Smith's behavior rather than statements of ideal behavior.

10. There are indications, however, that when it comes to the actual marriages of their children, parents take other factors into account. For example, it was said that one woman refused to allow her daughter to marry a young man, although he was regarded as a correct partner, because he was running around with other women. The girl's father's sister, on the other hand, urged her sister-in-law to consent to the marriage because the young man was straight. Eventually the girl's mother gave her consent. Another woman who had stressed the importance of a straight marriage for her eldest daughter, and who had consented to her daughter's choice of a straight partner, said she did not want her daughter to marry until she had finished school. The extent to which such considerations played a part in past bestowals of mothers-in-law and wives is unknown. The women I spoke to on the subject of mother-in-law bestowal denied that factors such as male aggressiveness or hunting ability played any role in partner selection—and indeed such factors would be irrelevant if bestowals were made to a four- or five-year-old child. It is likely, however, that at times, females were bestowed on older males, as, for example, might be the case when girls were bestowed as wives. In these circumstances, considerations of a man's ability or personality may have played a role in his selection as a future son-in-law. L. R. Hiatt, for example, says that Gidjingali bestowers consider the age of potential husbands (Hiatt 1965, 82). According to Ronald Berndt, in Northeast Arnhem Land the parents of a girl might take her away from a man who did not live up to their economic expectations (1965b, 85). Warren Shapiro tells of a case in which a man was "shamed" into bestowing one of his daughters by the generosity of a suitor (1981, 56). However, in both of the latter two cases at least one of the bestowers was a man. It is possible that male and female bestowers use different criteria or weigh criteria differently.

11. In 1978 there were also five such cases where the target of aggression was a young boy. In 1981 I recorded only one case where a young boy was the target. In this case a man threw spears at a young married man for running around with his daughter. (See chap. 2 for a discussion of the married status of some young boys.)

12. Sending such messages via a third party is not a new courting procedure (see, for example, Berndt 1951b). Sending letters, of course, has only become possible with literacy.

13. In many parts of Australia, a pregnant woman's husband dreams of the child his wife will bear, directing the child to its mother (Shapiro 1979, 9–10). As an apparent consequence, in Northeast Arnhem Land a child "refers to his father as his finder" and a man "refers to his child as 'one whom I found'" (Shapiro 1979, 10). At Mangrove,

where men do not usually dream their own children (see Chap. 2, n. 9), women used the word "find" in reference to children they have borne. They may also refer to a man as the one who "found" a child (Burbank 1980, 51).

14. The following year, Marguerite gave birth to a daughter. There was no mention of a marriage in the letter.

15. When one is asked for something at Mangrove, a more acceptable response is to say one has none than to refuse the request.

16. I know of only one other premarital pregnancy for the population at Mangrove. It occurred in 1957 and did not end in marriage to the child's father.

17. The marital status of the remaining two women is unknown as they were not living at Mangrove in 1981.

18. A mother's refusal to consent to a daughter's chosen match may be due to such a situation. Lily, for example, may have been unable to allow Marguerite to marry another because her promise refused to relinquish Marguerite altogether, even though she would not join him in a de facto union.

19. I have not included these five women in the sample of fifty-five young girls.

CHAPTER 5: CONCLUSION

1. As the only other group of recently settled hunters and gatherers studied as a part of the Harvard Adolescence Project, the Copper Inuit at Holman provide a particularly appropriate comparison for the situation at Mangrove. When this volume was still a manuscript in final preparation, only one of the ethnographies from the project was completed and in print. It is fortunate that this was Richard Condon's *Inuit Youth* (1987).

2. A further example of the flexible application of kin terms was provided by Nora, who told me that if there was too much "growling" between people who called each other *gajali* (mother-in-law/son-in-law), they might instead call each other *gagu* ("MM/DC"). Presumably, the change of terms implies that such women would not give their daughters to their now former sons-in-law. Also see Shapiro 1981, 137–138, and Shaw 1981, 59–60.

3. For example, an early missionary wrote in a report: "The native people still live in their own way, but with the constant teaching, especially of the children, we naturally expect results in due course" (quoted in Cole 1982, 34).

■ References

Agar, M. 1973. *Ripping and Running: A Formal Ethnography of Urban Heroin Addicts.* New York: Seminar Press.

Altman, J. 1984. "Hunter-Gatherer Subsistence Production in Arnhem Land: The Original Affluence Hypothesis Re-Examined." *Mankind* 14:179–190.

Barnard, A. 1983. "Contemporary Hunter-Gatherers: Current Theoretical Issues in Ecology and Social Organization." *Annual Review of Anthropology* 12:193–214.

Bauer, F. 1964. *Historical Geography of White Settlement in Part of Northern Australia, part 2: The Katherine-Darwin Region.* Canberra: Commonwealth Scientific and Industrial Research Organization.

Bayton, J. 1965. *Cross over Carpentaria: Being a History of the Church of England in Northern Australia from 1865–1965.* Brisbane: W. R. Smith and Paterson.

Bell, D. 1980. "Desert Politics: Choices in the 'Marriage Market.'" In M. Etienne and E. Leacock, eds., *Women and Colonization: Anthropological Perspectives.* New York: Praeger.

———. 1983. *Daughters of the Dreaming.* Sydney: McPhee Gribble/George Allen and Unwin.

Bell, D., and P. Ditton. 1980. *Law: The Old and The New: Aboriginal Women in Central Australia Speak Out.* Canberra: Aboriginal History.

Bern, J. 1979. "Ideology and Domination: Toward a Reconstruction of Australian Aboriginal Social Formation." *Oceania* 50:118–132.

Berndt, C. 1950. *Women's Changing Ceremonies in Northern Australia.* Paris: L'Homme.

Berndt, R. 1951a. *Kunapipi.* Melbourne: F. W. Cheshire.

———. 1951b. *Sexual Behavior in Western Arnhem Land.* New York: Viking Fund Publication in Anthropology.

_____. 1965a. "Law and Order in Aboriginal Australia." In R. Berndt, ed., *Aboriginal Man in Australia*. London: Angus Robertson.

_____. 1965b. "Marriage and the Family in North-Eastern Arnhem Land." In M. Nimkoff, ed., *Comparative Family Systems*. Boston: Houghton Mifflin.

Biernoff, D. 1974. "Pre and Post European Design of Aboriginal Settlements: The Case of the Nunggubuyu of Eastern Arnhem Land." *Man-Environment Systems* 4:273–282.

_____. 1979. "Traditional and Contemporary Structures and Settlement in Eastern Arnhem Land with Particular Reference to the Nunggubuyu." In M. Heppell, ed., *A Black Reality*. Canberra: Australia Institute of Aboriginal Studies.

_____. 1982. "Psychiatric and Anthropological Interpretations of 'Aberrant' Behavior in an Aboriginal Community." In J. Reid, ed., *Body, Land, and Spirit: Health and Healing in Aboriginal Society*. St. Lucia: University of Queensland Press.

Brady, M., and R. Morice. 1982. "Defiance or Despair? Petrol-Sniffing in an Aboriginal Community." In J. Reid, ed., *Body, Land, and Spirit: Health and Healing in Aboriginal Society*. St. Lucia: University of Queensland Press.

Broude, G. 1975. "Norms of Premarital Sexual Behavior." *Ethos* 3: 381–402.

_____. 1981. "The Cultural Management of Sexuality." In R. Munroe, R. Munroe, and J. Whiting, eds., *Handbook of Cross-Cultural Human Development*. New York: Garland Press.

Buckler, J. 1979. *A Reference Manual of Growth and Development*. Oxford: Blackwell.

Burbank, V. 1980. "Expressions of Anger and Aggression in an Australian Aboriginal Community." Ph.D. diss., Department of Anthropology, Rutgers University, New Brunswick, N.J.

_____. 1985. "The Mirriri as Ritualized Aggression." *Oceania* 56:47–55.

_____. 1987. "Premarital Sex Norms: Cultural Interpretations in an Australian Aboriginal Community." *Ethos* 15:226-234.

Capell, A. 1960. "Myths and Tales of the Nungguguyu, Southeast Arnhem Land." *Oceania* 31:31–62.

Colby, B. 1966. "The Analysis of Cultural Content and the Patterning of Narrative Concern in Texts." *American Anthropologists* 68: 374–388.

Cole, K. 1977. "A Critical Appraisal of Anglican Mission Policy and Practice in Arnhem Land, 1908–1939." In R. Berndt, ed., *Aborigines and Change: Australia in the 70s*. Canberra: Australian Institute of Aboriginal Studies.

_____. 1982. *A History of Numbulwar: The Story of an Aboriginal Community in Eastern Arnhem Land, 1952–1982*. Bendigo, Victoria: Keith Cole Publications.

Collier, J., and M. Rosaldo. 1981. "Politics and Gender in Simple Societies." In S. Ortner and H. Whitehead, eds., *Sexual Meanings: The Cultural Construction of Gender and Sexuality*. Cambridge: Cambridge University Press.

Condon, R. 1987. *Inuit Youth: Growth and Change in the Canadian Arctic*. New Brunswick, N.J.: Rutgers University Press.

Coombs, H., B. Dexter, and L. Hiatt. 1980. "The Outstation Movement in Aboriginal Australia." *Australian Institute of Aboriginal Studies Newsletter*, n. s. no. 14.

Cowlishaw, G. 1979. "Women's Realm: A Study of Socialization, Sexuality, and Reproduction among Australian Aborigines." Ph.D. diss., Department of Anthropology, University of Sydney, Sydney.

Daly, M., and M. Wilson. 1983. *Sex, Evolution, and Behavior: Adaptations for Reproduction*. Boston: Willard Grant.

D'Andrade, R. 1984. "Cultural Meaning Systems." In R. Shweder and R. LeVine, eds., *Culture Theory: Essays on Mind, Self, and Emotion*. Cambridge: Cambridge University Press.

Eckermann, A. K. 1977. "Group Organization and Identity within an Urban Aboriginal Community." In R. Berndt, ed., *Aborigines and Change: Australia in the 70s*. Canberra: Australian Institute of Aboriginal Studies.

Elkin, A. 1964. *The Australian Aborigines*. Garden City, N.Y.: Doubleday.

Eveleth, P., and J. Tanner. 1975. *World-Wide Variation in Human Growth*. Cambridge University Press.

Frisch, R., A. Gotz-Welbergen, J. McArthur, T. Albright, J. Witschi, B. Bullen, J. Birnholz, R. Reed, and H. Hermann. 1981. "Delayed Menarche and Amenorrhea of College Athletes in Relation to Age of Onset of Training." *Journal of the American Medical Association* 246:1559–1563.

Gale, F. 1970. "The Impact of Urbanization on Aboriginal Marriage Patterns." In R. Berndt, ed., *Australian Aboriginal Anthropology: Modern Studies in the Social Anthropology of the Australian Aborigine*. Nedlands, Western Australia: University of Western Australia Press.

Gonzales, N. 1970. "Toward a Definition of Matrifocality." In N. Whitten and J. Szwed, eds., *Afro-American Anthropology: Contemporary Perspectives*. New York: Free Press.

_____. 1984. "Rethinking the Consanguineal Household and Matrifocality." *Ethnology* 23:1–12.

Goodale, J. 1971. *Tiwi Wives*. Seattle: University of Washington Press.

Goodenough, W. 1970. *Description and Comparison in Cultural Anthropology.* Chicago: Aldine.

———. 1971. *Culture, Language, and Society.* Addison-Wesley Module 7. Reading, Mass.: Addison-Wesley.

Hamilton, A. 1974. "The Role of Women in Aboriginal Marriage Arrangements." In F. Gale, ed., *Woman's Role in Aboriginal Society.* Canberra: Australian Institute of Aboriginal Studies.

———. 1975. "Aboriginal Women: The Means of Production." In J. Mercer, ed., *The Other Half: Women in Australian Society.* Harmondsworth, England: Penguin.

———. 1980–1981. "Dual Social Systems: Technology, Labour and Women's Secret Rites in the Eastern Western Desert of Australia." *Oceania* 51:4–19.

———. 1981. *Nature and Nurture: Aboriginal Child-Rearing in North-Central Arnhem Land.* Canberra: Australian Institute of Aboriginal Studies.

Harris, S. 1980. *Culture and Learning: Tradition and Education in North East Arnhem Land.* Darwin: Northern Territory Department of Education.

Hart, C., and A. Pilling. 1960. *The Tiwi of North Australia.* New York: Holt, Rinehart, and Winston.

Heath, J. 1978. *Linguistic Diffusion in Arnhem Land.* Canberra: Australian Institute of Aboriginal Studies.

———. 1980. *Nunggubuyu Myths and Ethnographic Texts.* Canberra: Australian Institute of Aboriginal Studies.

Hiatt, B. 1974. "Woman the Gatherer." In F. Gale, ed., *Woman's Role in Aboriginal Society.* Canberra: Australian Institute of Aboriginal Studies.

Hiatt, L. 1965. *Kinship and Conflict: A Study of an Aboriginal Community in Northern Arnhem Land.* Canberra: Australia National University Press.

———. 1967. "Authority and Reciprocity in Australian Marriage Arrangements." *Mankind* 6:468–475.

———. 1968. "Gidjingali Marriage Arrangements." R. Lee and I. DeVore, ed., *Man the Hunter.* Chicago: Aldine.

———. 1985. "Maidens, Males, and Marx: Some Contrasts in the Work of Frederick Rose and Claude Meillassoux." *Oceania* 56: 34–46.

Hughes, E. 1971. *Nunggubuyu-English Dictionary.* Sydney: Oceania Linguistic Monographs, University of Sydney.

Irons, W. 1983. "Human Female Reproductive Strategies." In S. Wasser, ed., *Social Behavior of Female Vertebrates.* New York: Academic Press.

Kaberry, P. 1939. *Aboriginal Woman: Sacred and Profane.* New York: Gordon Press.

Keen, I. 1982. "How Some Murngin Men Marry Ten Wives: The Marital Implications of Matrilateral Cross-Cousin Structures:" *Man* 18:620–642.

———. 1986. "New Perspectives on Yolngu Affinity: A Review Article." *Oceania* 56:218–230.

Keesing, R. 1974. "Theories of Culture." *Annual Review of Anthropology* 3:73–97.

Kluckhohn, C. 1953. "Universal Categories of Culture," In A. Kroeber, ed., *Anthropology Today: An Encyclopedic Inventory.* Chicago: University of Chicago Press.

Koepping, K. P. 1977. "Cultural Patterns in an Aboriginal Settlement in Queensland." In R. Berndt, ed., *Aborigines and Change: Australia in the 70s.* Canberra: Australian Institute of Aboriginal Studies.

Kohlberg, L. 1981. "Indoctrination versus Relativity in Value Education." In L. Kohlberg, ed., *Essays in Moral Development,* vol. 1: *The Philosophy of Moral Development: Moral Stages and The Idea of Justice.* San Francisco: Harper and Row.

Kroeber, A. 1952. "Basic and Secondary Patterns of Social Structure." In A. Kroeber, ed., *The Nature of Culture.* Chicago: University of Chicago.

Lancaster, J. 1986. "Human Adolescence and Reproduction: An Evolutionary Perspective." In J. Lancaster and B. Hamburg, eds., *School-Age Pregnancy and Parenthood: Biosocial Dimensions.* Chicago: Aldine de Gruyter.

Leeden, van der, A. 1975. "Thundering Gecko and Emu: Mythological Structuring of Nunggubuyu Patrimoieties." In L. Hiatt, ed., *Australian Aboriginal Mythology.* Canberra: Australian Institute of Aboriginal Studies.

Lévi-Strauss, C. 1949. *The Elementary Structures of Kinship.* Boston: Beacon Press.

Lutz, C., and G. White. 1986. "The Anthropology of Emotions." *Annual Review of Anthropology* 15:405–436.

Maddock, K. 1969. "Alliance and Entailment in Australian Marriage." *Mankind* 7:19–26.

———. 1972. *The Australian Aborigines: A Portrait of Their Society.* Ringwood, Victoria: Pelican.

Malinowski, B. 1963. *The Family among the Australian Aborigines: A Sociological Study.* New York: Schocken Books.

Mead, M. 1928. *Coming of Age in Samoa.* New York: William Morris.

Meggitt, M. 1962. *Desert People: A Study of the Walbiri Aborigines of Central Australia*. Sydney: Angus and Robertson.

———. 1965. "Marriage among the Walbiri of Central Australia: A Statistical Examination." In R. Berndt and C. Berndt, eds., *Aboriginal Man in Australia*. Sydney: Angus and Robertson.

———. 1966. "Indigenous Forms of Government among the Australian Aborigines." In I. Hogbin and L. Hiatt, eds., *Readings in Australian and Pacific Anthropology*. Melbourne: Melbourne University Press.

Merlan, F. 1978. "Making People Quiet in the Pastoral North: Reminiscences of Elsey Station." *Aboriginal History* 2:70:105.

———. 1986. "Gender Review." Paper presented at the Australian Institute of Aboriginal Studies Biennial Conference, May 1986.

———. N.d. "Australian Aboriginal Conception Beliefs Revisited." University of Sydney. Typescript.

Money, J., J. Cawte, G. Bianchi, and B. Nurcombe. 1970. "Sex Training and Traditions in Arnhem Land." *British Journal of Medical Psychology* 43:383–399.

Montagu, A. 1979. *Reproductive Development of the Female*. Littleton, Mass.: P.S.G. Publishing.

Murdock, G. 1949. *Social Structure*. New York: Free Press.

———. 1968. "Discussions, part 7: Are the Hunter-Gatherers a Cultural Type." In R. Lee and I. DeVore, eds., *Man the Hunter*. Chicago: Aldine.

Myers, F. 1979. "Emotions and the Self: A Theory of Personhood and Political Order among Pintupi Aborigines." *Ethos* 7:343–370.

———. 1980a. "A Broken Code: Pintupi Political Theory and Contemporary Social Life." *Mankind* 12:311–326.

———. 1980b. "The Cultural Basis of Politics in Pintupi Life." *Mankind* 12:197–214.

Needham, R. 1986. "Alliance." *Oceania* 56:165–180.

Peterson, N. 1974. "The Importance of Women in Determining the Composition of Residential Groups in Aboriginal Australia." In F. Gale, ed., *Women's Role in Aboriginal Society*. Canberra: Australian Institute of Aboriginal Studies.

Piddington, R. 1970. "Irregular Marriages in Australia." *Oceania* 40:329–343.

Radcliffe-Brown, A. 1931. "The Social Organization of Australian Tribes." *Oceania* 1:426–456.

Reid, J. 1983. *Sorcerers and Healing Spirits: Continuity and Change in an Aboriginal Medical System*. Canberra: Australian National University Press.

Richardson, D., and R. Short. 1978. "Time of Onset of Sperm Production in Boys." *Journal of Biosocial Science Supplment* 5:15–26.

Rosaldo, M. 1980. "The Use and Abuse of Anthropology." *Signs* 5: 389–417.

Rose, F. 1960. *Classification of Kin, Age Structure, and Marriage amongst the Groote Eylandt Aborigines.* Berlin: Akademie-Verlag.

———. 1968. "Australian Marriage, Land-Owning Groups, and Initiations." In R. Lee and I. DeVore, eds., *Man the Hunter.* Chicago: Aldine.

Sackett, L. 1975–1976. "Exogamy or Endogamy: Kinship and Marriage at Wiluna, Western Australia." *Anthropological Forum* 4: 44–55.

———. 1976. "Indirect Exchange in a Symmetrical System: Marriage Alliance in the Western Desert of Australia." *Ethnology* 15: 135–149.

———. 1978. "Punishment as Ritual: 'Man-Making' among Western Desert Aborigines." *Oceania* 49:110–127.

Schlegel, A. 1983. "The Universality of Adolescence: An Anthropological Perspective." Paper presented at the Symposium on Rethinking Education and Socialization in the Third World. Eighty-third annual meeting of the American Anthropological Association, Chicago.

Shapiro, W. 1970. "Local Exogamy and the Wife's Mother in Aboriginal Australia." In R. Berndt, ed., *Australian Aboriginal Anthropology.* Nedlands: University of Western Australia Press.

———. 1973. "Residential Groupings in Northeast Arnhem Land." *Man* 8:365–383.

———. 1977. "Structure, Variation and Change in Balamumu Social Classification." *Journal of Anthropological Research* 33: 16–49.

———. 1979. *Social Organization in Aboriginal Australia.* New York: St. Martins Press.

———. 1981. *Miwuyt Marriage: The Cultural Anthropology of Affinity in Northeast Arnhem Land.* Philadelphia: Institute for the Study of Human Issues.

Shaw, B. 1981. *My Country of the Pelican Dreaming: The Life of an Australian Aborigine of the Gadjerong, Grant Ngabidj, 1904–1977.* Canberra: Australian Institute of Aboriginal Studies.

Short, R. 1976. "Definition of the Problem: The Evolution of Human Reproduction." *Proceedings of the Royal Society, London* 195: 3–24.

Stack, C. 1974. *All Our Kin: Strategies for Survival in a Black Community.* New York: Harper and Row.

Stanner, W. 1965. "The Dreaming." In W. Lessa and E. Vogt, eds., *Reader in Comparative Religion.* New York: Harper.

Sturmer, J. von. 1981. "Talking with Aborigines." *Australian Institute of Aboriginal Studies Newsletter,* n. s. no. 15.

Tanner, J. 1978. *Fetus into Man: Physical Growth from Conception to Maturity.* Cambridge: Harvard University Press.

Thompson, D. 1935–1936. "Interim General Report of Preliminary Expedition to Arnhem Land, Northern Territory of Australia."

Tindale, N. 1925–1926. "Natives of Groote Eylandt and of the West Coast of the Gulf of Carpentaria." *Records of the Southern Australian Museum* 3:61–102.

Tonkinson, R. 1978. *The Mardudjara Aborigines: Living the Dream in Australia's Desert.* New York: Holt, Rinehart and Winston.

Turner, D. 1974. *Tradition and Transformation: A Study of Aborigines in the Groote Eylandt Area, Northern Australia.* Canberra: Australian Institute of Aboriginal Studies.

———. 1980. *Australian Aboriginal Social Organization.* Canberra: Australian Institute of Aboriginal Studies.

Wallace, N. 1977. "Change in Spiritual and Ritual Life in Pitjantjatjara (Bidjandjadjara) Society, 1966 to 1973." In R. Berndt, ed., *Aborigines and Change: Australia in the '70s.* Canberra: Australian Institute of Aboriginal Studies.

Warner, W. 1937. *A Black Civilization: A Study of an Australian Tribe.* New York: Harper.

———. 1969. *A Black Civilization.* Rev. ed. Gloucester, Mass.: Peter Smith.

Webb, T. 1944. *From Spears to Spades.* Melbourne: Book Depot.

White, C., and N. Peterson. 1969. "Ethnographic Interpretations of the Prehistory of Western Arnhem Land." *Southwestern Journal of Anthropology* 25:45–66.

White, I. 1974. "Aboriginal Women's Status: A Paradox Resolved.' In F. Gale, ed., *Woman's Role in Aboriginal Society.* Canberra: Australian Institute of Aboriginal Studies.

———. 1975. "Sexual Conquest and Submission in the Myths of Central Australia." In L. Hiatt, ed., *Australian Aboriginal Mythology.* Canberra: Australian Institute of Aboriginal Studies.

Whitehead, T. 1978. "Residence, Kinship, and Mating as Survival Strategies: A West Indian Example." *Journal of Marriage and the Family* 39:817–827.

Whiting, J. 1968. "Methods and Problems in Cross:Cultural Research." In L. Lindzey and E. Aronson, eds., *The Handbook of Social Psychology,* 2d ed. Reading, Mass.: Addison-Wesley.

Whiting, J., V. Burbank, and M. Ratner. 1982. "The Duration of Maidenhood." Paper presented at Social Science Research Council Conference on School-Age Pregnancy and Parenthood, Elkridge, Md.

―――. 1986. "The Duration of Maidenhood." In J. Lancaster and B. Hamburg, eds., *School-Age Pregnancy and Parenthood: Biosocial Dimensions*. Chicago: Aldine.

Whiting, J., and B. Whiting. 1975. "Aloofness and Intimacy of Husbands and Wives: A Cross-Cultural Study." *Ethos* 3:183–208.

Woodburn, J. 1980. "Hunters and Gatherers Today and Reconstruction of the Past." In E. Gellner, ed., *Soviet and Western Anthropology*. London: Duckworth.

Worsley, P. 1954. "The Changing Social Structure of the Wanindiljaugwa." Australian National University. Typescript.

Young, E. 1980. "Numbulwar: From Mission Station to Aboriginal Community." Development Studies Centre, Research School of Pacific Studies, Australian National University. Typescript.

Zacharias, L., and R. Wurtman. 1969. "Age at Menarche: Genetic and Environmental Influences." *New England Journal of Medicine* 280:868–875.

■ Index

abandonment by husband, 88–89, 90–91, 97

abduction of girl, promise and, 66

Aboriginal Council, 15, 39

adolescent females: abduction of, 66; age concept and, 10–11; demographic analysis and, 19; labels for, 4; maidenhood concept and, 4–6, 115, 116, 118–119; negative attitude toward marriage and, 92–98; peer support and, 104–107; regulation of sexual behavior of, 6–7; school and, 22; sexual experience of, 83; work and, 23, 24, 25. *See also* females; marriage; promise (betrothal)

adolescent males: analysis of boys and, 31–33; education of (into ritual knowledge), 35–38; social control of, 33–34. *See also* boys; males

adolescents: children and end of stage of, 10; daily routine of, 26–29; disruptive behavior of, 39–40; as invention of settlement life, 17; life stage of (at settlement), 4; strategies con-

cerning marriage and, 104–107; strategies concerning marriage case histories and, 107–113; Western culture and, 43; work and, 23–26. *See also* adolescent females; adolescent males

adultery: adolescent female's expectations and, 89–90; adult females and, 97–98; male showing off and, 93–94; young men and, 33–34. *See also* sexual behavior

adults: conflict over marriage and, 101–102, 114; marriage strategies and, 102–104; in study, 11

Afro-Americans, 121

afternoon siesta, 28

age: contemporary marriage and, 60–61; demographic shifts and, 19; girls and Aboriginal concept of, 10–11; of marriage, 32, 55–56, 118; mission and marriage, 65–66; polygynous marriage and, 60; of school children, 20; of study informants, 10; views on marriage and, 116

basic roles of, 119–120; ceremonies of the Law and, 31;
concept of "unmarried," 110–
111, 119–120; as co-wives,
121, 123; "exchange" and, 49,
54–55; fear of men and, 86;
food production and, 122; ideal
marriage age for, 55–56; labor
of, 47; male aggression toward,
96–97; marriage analysis and,
46–47, 49, 50–51; "purchase"
of young (by missionaries), 61;
smoko and, 26; work and, 23,
25. *See also* adolescent females
fishing, 27
food: bestowal and obligation for,
58; breakfast, 26; daily routine
of adolescents and, 26; females
and production of, 122; lunch,
27; preparation of evening
meal and, 28; *smoko* (morning
tea) and, 26–27
funeral dancing, 8

gajali. See promise (betrothal)
gambling, 26, 27, 28 29, 40
Goodale, J., 56
Groot Eylandt Aborigines, 32, 35,
55, 59, 69
Gsell, Father, 61
guardianship, 35

Hamilton, A., 122
Hansen's disease, 111
happiness, 91–92
Hart, C. W. M., 47, 50
health problems, 111
Hiatt, L. R., 47
Holman (Canada), 116–118
hostility: adolescent girls and
adult women and, 99; male
(toward females), 96–97;

marriage choice and intergenerational, 103–104
household chores, 22
household composition, 16, 17,
18, 120–123
housing: residential arrangements and, 17–19; in study
settlement, 14, 15
hunting, 23, 28

infant mortality, 19
infidelity. *See* adultery
informants (study), 7–11
initiation, 31, 33; ritual knowledge and, 36, 37
intergenerational conflict, 98–
100, 103–104
interviews; marriage behavior,
79–84; study, 7–11
Inuit (Canadian Arctic) community, 116–118

Jane's dilemma (marriage expectations example), 79–84,
85–86, 96, 97, 99–100, 101,
105, 107, 125
jealousy, 90
jobs. *See* occupations; work

Kaberry, P., 120
kinship: classification system
and, 29; kin terms and, 30–
31; marriage and, 47–48;
social organization and, 29
Kriol (Aboriginal language). *See*
language
Kroeber, A., 50

Lancaster, J., 6
language: in school (Kriol and
English), 20; study and Kriol,
11; terms in Aboriginal (Kriol),
4